W9-ATM-612

In an entertaining yet realistic format, the authors share practical advice for turning the bitter parent/child power struggle into a healthy, wholesome relationship. After reading this book, you will want to keep it as a ready reference to revisit again and again. The next time you are faced with the "who's in charge?" challenge from your child, you will be equipped to respond quickly and confidently. I highly recommend it!

JERRY HADDOCK, ED.D.
Southern California Regional Director
Association of Christian Schools International

Children instinctively know when to strike in challenging a parent's authority. Holt and Dodson have given us serveral such parenting scenarios with both the right and wrong way to respond as parents for our instruction in wise parenting practices. This book is a gold mine of practical help for the parent who truly wants to do the job right.

Every parent will be able to identify with the practical scenarios that our authors have chosen. In a day where we have lost our spiritual moorings, this book will challenge and encourage parents to handle their God-given responsibility with wisdom.

JIM WELLES
Pastor of Children's Ministry
Crossroads Baptist Church
Bellevue, Washington

Permissiveness and trying too hard to keep children happy are major mistakes in parenting today. Holt and Dodson have come together with an effective antidote for these toxins!

GRACE KETTERMAN, M.D.
Psychiatrist and author

This book reaffirms an old lesson: Parents have more effect on their children than they realize. It will make you more of a thinking parent. As a result, your kids will learn how to think and communicate better about relationships.

ANDREW G. HODGES, M.D.
Psychiatrist and author

For those of us who have ever loved a child enough to help with homework, take him or her out to eat, or participate in other caring, training opportunities, this book is worthwhile. Practical, step-by-step advice leaves the reader thinking, "Absolutely! This makes sense." Totally usable information.

MARLENE LEFEVER
Author of *Learning Styles—Reaching Everyone God Gave You to Teach*

Your Kids Have a Plan... Do You?

Illustrated by TODD SHAFFER

Pat Holt & Lori Dodson

Tyndale House Publishers, Inc.
WHEATON · ILLINOIS

Library of Congress Cataloging-in-Publication Data

Holt, Pat,   date
  Your kids have a plan . . . do you? / Pat Holt and Lori Dodson.
      p.   cm.
  Includes index.
  ISBN 0-8423-4984-7 (sc : alk, paper)
  1. Parent and child. 2. Parent and child—Religious aspects—Christianity.   3. Child
rearing.   4. Child rearing—Religious aspects—Christianity.   I. Dodson, Lori, date.   II. Title.
HQ755.85.H634   1997
649′.1—dc20   96-19073

Printed in the United States of America

01   00   99   98   97
7   6   5   4   3   2   1

CONTENTS

A VERY IMPORTANT NOTE TO PARENTS

Dear Mom and Dad,

For many years, we have watched parents who love their children dearly, who would sacrifice anything and everything for them, experience increasing frustration. They are well-meaning parents but, too often, their results are disappointing and leave them with a growing sense of helplessness.

We have watched as men and women are transformed from adoring, doting parents into people who are ridden with anxiety, wondering what will happen next. The only things they are sure of are that they probably will be unable to cope, they may do the wrong thing, and they might even fail—miserably.

These parents are baffled as to how it all happened—and so early! How did an adorable person under three feet tall become the demanding ruler of their home?

That is the bit of very bad news. But now, for the really good news:

There are some simple, basic principles, which we refer to as "clues for Christian parents," that can transform you from a hesitant, anxious, and frustrated parent into a parent who is confident, capable, and joyful. The prayerful, consistent application of these principles—infallible because they come from God's Word—is the key to successful parenting.

To make the process more vivid, we will "show" rather than "tell" what happens when the child is in control and how that control propels a parent-child power struggle. Each chapter will look at a different child-rearing challenge, which we think will be familiar to you. For each one, we'll give numerous clues for Christian parents and answer some commonly asked questions. Then we will demonstrate the identical problem handled with the parent in control, showing how you can diffuse the parent-child power struggle.

The situations we have selected to illustrate are common to all families. Although Jason, our main character, is of early school age, the child-rearing principles demonstrated and discussed apply equally well to training a toddler or a teen. Similarly, the principles hold true regardless of your specific family circumstances—whether your family is a two-original-parent home, a blended family, an extended family, a family in transition, or a single-parent family.

Let's get started, and let's have some smiles along the way!

Because of *his* love,
Lori and Pat

SPECIAL NOTE
TO SINGLE PARENTS

It is a special blessing when a child has two parents in the home who are united in their love for the Lord and in their discipline standards. However, nothing is too hard for the Lord, according to Genesis 18:14, and God is all-powerful. Isaiah 61:3 assures a parent that God can take the ashes of any home situation, and "he will give beauty for ashes, joy instead of mourning, praise instead of despair."

Many of the heroes of the Bible did not have "normal" home lives. Reading about the childhood of Moses, Joseph, Samuel, Jonathan, Daniel, Esther, or Gideon will comfort any parent who is not able to provide an "ideal" situation. God delights in showing his great love and in overcoming power in situations that are "impossible" when seen through human eyes.

What God does require of a parent who loves him is to "bring [your children] up with the discipline and instruction approved by the Lord" (Ephesians 6:4) and "to do what is right, to love mercy, and to walk humbly with your God" (Micah 6:8). All of the principles for parents explained in "before and after" detail in this book are a part of doing what is right, loving mercy, and walking humbly—and they are all equally applicable and effective whether enforced by two loving parents or one.

Whether your family is united, broken, or blended, as you cry out to God for the wisdom, patience, and consistency to do the job of parenting "as though you were working for the Lord" (Colossians 3:23), God will give encouragement. Trust the Lord to be faithful, to give what is needed when it is needed (and as much as is needed) to raise a child who will grow to be an adult of strong, Christian character.

CHOICES

The embarrassing but
all–too–familiar parent–child
power struggle in a restaurant

*Parents who neglect discipline are
their children's worst enemies.*

E. MARION DICK

*The godly walk with integrity;
blessed are their children after them.*

PROVERBS 20:7

JASON IN CHARGE

Jason and his parents are going out for dinner. Here's Jason's perspective on it:

"My mom and dad and I are going out to dinner tonight. I want to go to a pizza place that has toys you can play on. But Mom says this time we have to go to a grown-up restaurant, and I'm supposed to act like a big boy. I hate it because Mom and Dad eat so slow and talk forever. It's *soooooo boring!*"

Clue for Christian Parents

Jason is set up for failure. His parents are set up for disappointment. It is obvious that Jason has experienced this type of situation before and did not like it. He does not want to be "grown up" or be challenged to "act like a big boy." He interprets both as "boring." His negative attitude implies two things: (1) This situation is not appropriate for Jason's behavioral age, and (2) Jason's parents have not laid the groundwork necessary to ensure a positive experience for Jason and for themselves.

"It's time to go, Jason," his mom says. "Go use the bathroom before we leave."

Jason goes down the hall, but before he makes it to the bathroom, he sees his trucks and starts playing with them. Soon Dad comes and says, "Jason, it's time to leave. Go get in the car."

"Aw, Dad," Jason laments, "I don't want to go to some stupid old restaurant. Why do I have to go, Dad?"

Dad responds with authority, "Because I said so. You do as I say, young man!"

Clue for Christian Parents

Whenever a parent tells a child "Do as I say" or orders obedience "just because I said so," that parent has laid the groundwork for a power struggle. But is there an alternative? What is a parent to do?

What does God do? From Genesis through Revelation, God sets standards, boundaries for behavior. But God has such love and respect for us who are created in his own image that he graciously allows us the power of choice. We can choose to obey, or we can choose to disobey. Because "the human heart is most deceitful and desperately wicked" (Jeremiah 17:9), God knows that to encourage good choices there must be the perks of positive and negative consequences.

Over and over again, God states to his willful people, "If you fully obey the Lord your God . . ." and then lists the blessings that will follow. Naturally, God never ignores bad behavior. God assures the children of Israel, "But if you refuse to listen to the Lord your God and do not obey . . ." and then gives the very unfortunate list of negative consequences that follow as a direct result of disobedience. (See

4

Deuteronomy 11:26-28 and Deuteronomy 28.)

God is consistent. We can always count on the blessings if we choose to obey. And we can always count on the loss of blessing and the negative consequences when we choose to disobey.

So then, what is a parent to do? God the Father has laid out a perfect pattern for us. Naturally, we want our children to obey out of hearts full of love, but since the heart is not pure but needs years of godly training, biblical counseling, and prayerful development, God's pattern works wonders in a home:

1. Clearly state the rules, making certain that they are simple enough to be understood and that there are not too many.
2. Explain the rules over and over in different ways at different times.
3. Let your child know that there is a choice—to obey or to disobey—and that the choice is the child's.
4. Let your child know exactly what the consequences of the behavior choice will be—both positive and negative. The child must clearly understand that if obedience is chosen, the positive consequence(s) will be such and such, but if the child chooses to disobey, then he or she will not only lose out on the positive consequence(s) but will face the negative consequence(s) as well.

The specific positive and negative consequences must be different for each child at each age and stage of development. That is why Christian parents must not only know their children but must also know the God who promises to give wisdom, discernment, guidance, direction, and the ability to be consistent!

Jason stomps down the hall running his hands along the wall.

Clue for Christian Parents
A child's negative body language is as powerful as words and deserves an immediate negative consequence.

In the car, Mom says, "Fasten your seat belt, Jason, and stop jumping around. You know you need to stay seated when Daddy's driving."

Jason buckles his seat belt, but not until Dad gives him a menacing glare in the rearview mirror.

Clue for Christian Parents
It is tragic to observe a parent allowing a child to make a series of poor choices without receiving appropriate negative consequences along the way. It is all too clear that God's pattern of discipline for parents to use with children is not in effect in this home. Unfortunately, because God is consistent and his Word is true, there will be negative consequences for the parents and the family because of their nonbiblical child-rearing choices.

The family walks into a packed restaurant. Dad goes up to give their name. Walking back to his wife, he says, "It's a forty-five-minute wait. Jason will be a bear. Maybe we should go somewhere else?"

"Oh, honey," Mom insists, "I've been looking forward to this. Can't we stay?"

"OK," Dad agrees, shrugging.

Sitting down to wait, Mom and Dad start talking to each other. "I want to go out and walk in the parking lot. It's too hot in here," Jason says loudly.

"No, sit still," Dad replies. Suddenly Dad realizes that Jason is kicking the seat and, in the process, kicks the leg of the lady next to him.

"Jason!" Dad says in astonishment. "Tell the lady you're sorry." Jason buries his head in the seat. Dad looks at the lady, smiles sheepishly, and says, "I'm terribly sorry."

Jason turns back around and starts kicking his feet again. Dad immediately places his hand on Jason's legs to still them. "I'm *hungry!* When are we gonna eat?!" Jason yells.

Mom sighs. "You'd better take him out. I'll listen for our name." Dad and Jason get up and go out to the parking lot.

Clue for Christian Parents
Children are so smart! Many times it seems that they are more skilled than parents in getting others to comply with

their demands. Your children are well aware that if they just make your life increasingly unpleasant, eventually you will give up and give in. Whenever this happens, your children have demonstrated that they are truly in charge of the family!

In this case, Jason is in total control of the situation. Jason has learned that he can manipulate his parents to achieve his own goals. He knew from previous experience that by not sitting still he could get Dad to comply with his desire to walk in the parking lot.

Finally, Mom opens the restaurant door and motions for them to come in. As soon as they're seated, Jason grabs a menu. "I don't see hot dogs on here. I want a hot dog!"

"Dear," Mom cajoles, "there are other things you will like. How about chicken?"

"I don't want chicken! *I want a hot dog!*" screams Jason. People from other tables are beginning to look at them.

Mom begins to sound irritated. "I told you there are no hot dogs, so you'll have to choose something else."

Jason scowls and looks back at his menu.

"I told you we shouldn't have brought him," Dad says to Mom as Jason listens.

Clue for Christian Parents

Parents must present a united front to their children. As soon as a child realizes that parents disagree on any issue, the child will quickly figure out how to play them against each other.

"I want psghetti and a Coke," Jason announces.

"Great!" Dad says with disgust. "I'm glad that's settled!"

"You need to have milk with dinner, Jason," Mom reminds him as the waitress comes over.

"What's your name, big boy?" the waitress asks with a pleasant smile.

"Jason!" Jason yells.

The smile fades. "What can I get you?" she asks routinely.

"I want psghetti and a Coke," Jason answers.

"Make that milk instead of Coke," corrects Mom.

"I don't want milk. I want Coke!" Jason insists.

"No, Jason, with dinner you know you must have milk," Mom tells him with all the firmness she can muster.

"I won't drink it!" Jason says decisively.

The waitress has wasted enough time. "I'll come back in a few minutes." She starts to leave.

Mom quickly looks to Dad for support. "No," Dad says with annoyed frustration, "just bring him a Coke."

Jason beams. "All right, Dad!"

Mom winces, then looks helpless and downcast. Dad wishes he weren't here.

Clue for Christian Parents

It really doesn't matter what Dad or Mom chooses; they're both going to lose. In fact, they've already lost. Either or both of these parents continually give up. Jason is the clear winner, and he knows it!

A child who is rewarded for repeated disobedience by getting his own willful way is a child who will keep on disobeying.

While waiting for the food, Jason turns around and bothers other diners. His parents are uncomfortable and unsure. Mom snaps at Jason, "Turn around this minute!" Jason ignores her. Then she snipes at her husband, "Can't you do something with him?"

Dad is plenty disgusted. He snarls, "I told you from the start it was a bad idea to bring him here, but you insisted. Now you can see what you've done!"

This conversation sounds interesting, so Jason turns around. His parents become silent. He knows they are angry with each other.

"Isn't the food ever coming?" Jason moans.

"We just have to be patient, dear," his mother cajoles.

"The higher the price, the longer the wait for the food. This is getting to be ridiculous," Dad fumes.

Now Jason jumps off the chair. First he walks around the table, touching the chairs. Then he begins to head toward other tables. His parents whisper loudly, "Get back here now, Jason!" He ignores them. Dad grumbles, gets up from the table, and grabs Jason. "Sit down in that chair and stay there!"

Clue for Christian Parents

Parents who are not a united team compound the difficulties of child rearing. Raising children "with the discipline and instruction approved by the Lord" (Ephesians 6:4) is a tough task even when parents *are* united. When parents are at odds with one another, anger and/or guilt—rather than the principles of the Word of God—determine the child-rearing strategies.

As soon as the food arrives, Jason announces that he needs to go to the bathroom. "Didn't you go before we left the house?" Mom asks.

"Yes," Jason lies, "but I need to go again."

"Well, that *was* over an hour ago," Mom says, rationalizing, as she looks at her watch, then at her husband.

"Now my food's going to be cold," Dad complains. As he gets up from the table, he angrily mutters to his wife, "Never again!"

This was not the relaxing dinner Mom had envisioned. The dinner has not been relaxing for the diners in close proximity, either. They are wondering why these people would bring this out-of-control boy to such a nice restaurant.

Jason comes running up to the table ahead of Dad. Heads turn in disgust. Jason plops down and begins to slurp his spaghetti and blow bubbles in his Coke. Bread crumbs and spaghetti are all over the table. In no time Jason is through and wants to go home. He starts crying loudly because Mom's taking too long.

Finally Dad says, "Let's just go!" As they get up to leave, Dad grabs Jason's arm just before he runs into a waitress carrying a tray of hot food.

"Never again!" Dad repeats angrily to Mom.

As they exit, there is an almost audible sigh of relief from the other diners.

Clue for Christian Parents
A child who misbehaves in a public place is an offense to others. The child-rearing problems of the parent(s) become the observers' problems, too. Their right to privacy is violated.

Yes, it happens all the time. That doesn't make it right. It is critical for Christian parents to model for others what God can do as the power of the Holy Spirit works through the Word and through prayer to mold the heart and mind of a child.

Q & A THAT LEAD THE WAY

Q: *At what age is a child old enough to take to a restaurant?*

A: When a child knows how to listen to parents and obey them. This also involves the child's being able to sit still and behave appropriately with good table manners for the length of time necessary for the particular restaurant you have selected. Activities such as turning around to bother other diners, loud talking, table-hopping, making sounds with the cutlery, sticking feet out to trip diners

12

and waitresses, etc. are totally inappropriate anytime and should never be permitted.

Basically, the "age"—or level of development—of the *parenting skills,* not the chronological age of the child, is the key determining factor. The disciplinary skills of some parents are so well developed that they are able to take a child under the age of two to a restaurant and leave with accolades. Then there are parents whose skills are so painfully underdeveloped that they cannot take a child of nine to a restaurant without acute discomfort to themselves and the other diners.

Q: *Was it OK for Jason to respond to Dad's direction by saying he didn't want to go to "some stupid old restaurant"?*

A: No, for two reasons. First, Dad did not ask Jason if he wanted to go. He gave him a direction to get into the car, which should have been obeyed.

Second, the word *stupid* is derogatory and should not be part of a child's normal vocabulary. Just because a child knows certain words and hears them in the neighborhood, at school, on TV, or perhaps even at church or while visiting Christian friends' homes does not make them appropriate. If the word or phrase is not honoring to the Lord, the wise parent will discuss this with the child and pray with the child, asking the Lord's help with self-control in this area.

Never condemn your child for knowing an inappropriate word or phrase. Your child needs to know that you have heard it all but choose not to use some words because they are not pleasing to the Lord. Your child also needs to know that you, too, have to ask the Lord for self-control in the area of language.

13

Help your child realize that not using the unkind or off-color words that "everybody else" uses can be a silent testimony for God. There are many instances where a child's "clean lips" give an opportunity to be a witness for Jesus. At an early age, children need to know that their behavior—verbal and nonverbal—is an important testimony for the Lord.

Q: *Should there be consequences of body language such as stomping feet or running hands along walls?*

A: Absolutely! Negative body language is a nonverbal form of rebellion.

Q: *Is it disobedient for a child to wait to be told to sit down in the car and fasten the seat belt?*

A: The majority of toddlers still need some help in fastening the seat belt. Most preschoolers (ages three and four) are old enough to do it by themselves. If children are old enough to do it by themselves, parents should expect them to get in the car, sit down, and buckle up immediately. Children should be taught that being a passenger in a car is serious business, and proper precautions for their safety and well-being must be taken automatically! If children are capable of sitting down and buckling up and don't do it, you can almost always assume it is an act of disobedience.

Q: *Dad knew when they had to wait to be seated that Jason's behavior would not be good. Should they have stayed and waited for a table?*

A: Before selecting a restaurant, Jason's parents needed to consider the full amount of time that would be involved.

The time it takes to get ready, drive to the restaurant, be seated, order, wait for the food, eat, pay, and get back home must all be considered in the total amount of time. It is also important to consider the bedtime of the child. Then you can determine whether such a time allotment is realistic for the behavioral age of your child. If not, you need to choose a different restaurant or make it an adult occasion rather than attempt a family time.

Actually, it was obvious by Jason's behavior from the beginning that his parents should never have taken him. The initial mistake was just compounded as the evening progressed. Jason was not trained to eat in a restaurant, and he certainly did not want to "dine out"!

The dilemma facing the family on this particular evening was a three-way power struggle. Mom wanted to eat in a certain restaurant. This put her in a power struggle with both her husband and Jason. Dad reluctantly succumbed to his wife's wishes, knowing full well what would happen. Then he lashed out at Jason in his frustrated anger and blamed Jason's behavior on the mother for selecting that restaurant. Jason made them both suffer. He had to go to a place he did not want to go, and he made them pay!

Q: *Should Jason have been required to apologize to the lady he inadvertently kicked?*

A: Yes. Jason should have been required to look her in the eye and tell her that he was sorry and that it would not happen again. Then he should have immediately apologized to his father for the bad attitude that led to his disobedience in kicking the seat. Such courtesy should be

15

common in a Christian family, even if it is becoming uncommon in our society.

Q: *Why did Dad let Jason have the Coke when Mom said he needed to order milk?*

A: Dad was looking for the easy way out. He wanted to salvage the evening and thought his decision would bring peace with Jason. Remember also that he was already plenty irritated with his wife for selecting this restaurant.

Frequently a parent believes that giving in on a small issue will make the child content. What a fantasy! Does the old saying "Give them an inch, and they'll take a mile" sound familiar? This is how it is when training children. Giving in to Jason allowed him to see the division between his parents and to assume control of the family in this situation.

Since Mom said Jason needed to order milk, Dad should have supported her decision. If he disagreed, he should have discussed it with her at another time and place without Jason present. Ideally, the matter of ordering a Coke or a glass of milk should have been decided and communicated to Jason long before the family entered the restaurant.

HOW TO REMOVE THE PARENT-CHILD POWER STRUGGLE IN A RESTAURANT

As soon as your child is feeding himself, it is time to teach table manners. Such basic manners as thanking God for the food before eating, chewing with the mouth closed, not talking with food in the mouth, sitting up straight, learning to use a napkin, not playing with food, not slurping, speaking in a pleasant tone of voice, staying in the chair, and waiting to be excused must be practiced meal by meal on a daily basis. And even a small child can be taught to clear dishes from the table.

If table manners are taught in the home, meal by meal, until they are an ingrained habit, then eating in a restaurant can be a happy family occasion for parents, children, waiters/waitresses, and fellow diners!

Let's rework the "going to a restaurant" scene with Mom and Dad united in their God-given position of authority in the family.

MOM AND DAD IN CHARGE

One night at the dinner table, Mom, Dad, and Jason are talking together about the events of each other's day. Mom casually mentions that friends have told her about a restaurant, one she would like to try as a family for dinner some night.

Dad picks up on the idea. "Sounds like fun, honey! Jason," he remarks with pleasure, "I've noticed how much more careful you've been lately with your table manners. You are remembering to chew with your mouth closed, and you're doing a much better job of not spilling your food or slurping." Dad teases, "I remember when you used to spill and slurp with every meal! Of course, you were younger and smaller then."

"I sure was, Dad! That was a very *l-o-n-g* time ago—even before my birthday!" Jason recalls with amazement.

Mom picks right up with the compliments. "You are also sitting like a big boy in your chair for a longer time than you used to, and I'm so proud of the way you are learning to use your napkin!"

Jason beams.

Clue for Christian Parents

Table manners are hard to learn. When children are at school (and often in the homes of other children), they are generally observing table behavior that says, "Shovel it in, and if it drops, so what? Let's get out of here and play!" Children who are trying to overcome such peer group role modeling need all the encouragement from parents and older siblings they can get!

Dad smiles. "Well, then, it's settled. Our big boy is ready for a night out with Mom and Dad!"

Clue for Christian Parents

Jason's dad handled this situation with kindness and wisdom. He was supportive and respectful of his wife's wish to try a new restaurant as a family. He wanted to prepare his son in such a way that Jason realized that going out with Mom and Dad to a restaurant was a reward for a job well done.

As an integral part of the family team, children need to know that going somewhere special with Mom and Dad is an earned privilege, not something unpleasant to be endured. That is, a child needs to realize that spending time with Mom and Dad in a restaurant is a special benefit of learning and practicing behavior skills that are not easy.

Each evening at dinner, the family discusses their upcoming "family night out" at the restaurant. Whenever possible, Mom and Dad reinforce the table-manner standards of behavior they have been patiently teaching and that Jason has been slowly—ever so slowly!—learning, meal by meal, day by day.

Clue for Christian Parents
It has been said that as much as 50 percent of the pleasure of an event is in the planning! The excitement mounts as the night out with Mom and Dad is discussed. With Mom and Dad's appropriate encouragement, a child is reassured of his or her ability to do the right thing at the right time. This type of praise increases confidence and removes anxiety from the child's thinking.

"Tonight is the big night out, Jason!" Dad announces just before he leaves for work.

"I'm so excited!" Mom responds.

Jason is also enthusiastic. "Me, too! I can hardly wait!"

"I'd like to go as early as possible," Dad adds, "before the restaurant gets crowded. I should know around noon whether I'll be able to leave early or not, and I'll give you a call."

"That's great," Mom says. "If you can't, I'll try to make reservations so we won't have to wait too long."

Clue for Christian Parents
When going out to dinner with children, wise parents try to go early. There is usually less of a wait, and it is best for the child's bedtime schedule. Making reservations is another way to prevent a long wait. Since many restaurants are less busy early in the week, going out on a Monday or Tuesday evening might also work well.

"Jason, I know you are ready, that you know what to do, and that you will do all the things we do at home," Dad begins.

"I sure will, Dad! You can count on me!"

Smiling, he continues, "I know that, Jason. Mom and I are

very proud of you. However, there may be children in that restaurant who don't know what to do."

Jason is surprised. "You mean their mommies and daddies haven't told them?"

"That's right, Jason, and sometimes it's because those mommies and daddies don't know how to train their children. So it is very important that we honor the Lord by setting a good example for the other families," Mom encourages.

"Let's have a time of prayer right now about our witness in the restaurant this evening," Dad suggests. They gather together, bow their heads, and close their eyes. Mom and Jason each pray, and Dad closes. They kiss, say their goodbyes, and Dad leaves.

Clue for Christian Parents
Parents of children who know how to behave in public have a responsibility to set an example for others. So do the children. However, this must never be done in a prideful I'll-show-you! manner. That is disgusting to other parents and not Christlike. In a humble manner, children and parents who know what to do and do it in public can be a powerful witness to other children and give hope and encouragement to other parents.

Jason can hardly wait for Dad to come home from work. By the time Dad walks into the house, Jason has cleaned up and is ready to go.

"Jason, we will be leaving the house in five minutes. Dad is just going to wash up and change his clothes. Please put away your toys and go to the bathroom. Remember to wash your hands," Mom requests.

Clue for Christian Parents
When you keep your child informed about an event, the child: (1) understands what is going on and why; (2) has a

more positive attitude toward the event because of this understanding; (3) gains assurance that he or she is an integral part of the family team; (4) feels proud to be worthy of the information; (5) begins to develop some understanding of how to plan and organize.

In about five minutes, Dad calls, "Come on, Jason, time to go. Let's get in the car."

Clue for Christian Parents
Jason's parents say what they mean and mean what they say. Jason has learned that they can be trusted.

Parents who know who God is and know his Word learn to trust him more. Children similarly grow in learning to trust earthly parents who say what they mean and mean what they say—in the smallest things of daily life as well as in the biggest things, in the positive rewards and in the negative consequences.

Jason gets into the backseat. Carefully he puts on his seat belt. As Dad starts the car, he smiles and winks at Jason in the rearview mirror. Jason grins broadly.

Clue for Christian Parents
Parents must be ever on the alert to praise a child for good behavior. Take every opportunity to legitimately praise a child both verbally and nonverbally.

At the restaurant, Jason takes Dad's hand. They go to put their name on the waiting list, while Mom sits in the waiting area.

Going back to Mom, Dad is pleased. "Only a ten-minute wait. That's not bad."

Jason sits between them, and they talk about the birthday party Jason went to yesterday. Dad talks about his week at work, and Mom shares the details of her busy week.

Clue for Christian Parents

A family time is a time when all members of the family share about the important events of their day or week. Including your child in the conversation teaches the child both verbal and listening skills. You need to model the difficult skill of listening without interrupting and be prepared to deal with children who interrupt.

At a family dinner, you must include children in the conversation. The events of their day should get equal time. They have stories that are saved up for dinnertime, and they deserve to be heard with full attention.

In about fifteen minutes, the family is seated. Jason remembers to say thank you to the waitress when she hands him a menu. Jason realizes that his parents noticed and smiled at him with approval.

Jason looks at the menu, hoping to find hot dogs. "What would you like, Jason?" Mom asks.

"I was hoping for a hot dog, but I don't see it."

Mom smiles. "No, they don't have hot dogs, Jason. How about chicken?"

Jason looks some more. "I think I'd like psghetti and a Coke."

"You'll need to have milk with dinner, Jason," Mom says.

Jason sighs and rolls his eyes. He looks at his dad for support.

Dad looks over the top of his menu at Jason with a commanding look of surprise. Not a word is spoken.

"Sorry, Mom. Sorry, Dad," Jason says.

Clue for Christian Parents

Parents who are united in their discipline of their child, with a commitment to fully supporting each other in the teaching of the principles of God's Word, automatically avoid much of the power-struggle problem that other children learn through observing the competitive power-struggle role modeling of their parents.

The waitress comes over to take their order. "What's your name, big boy?" she asks.

Jason looks at her and clearly responds, "Jason."

"What'll it be, Jason?" she asks.

"I'll have psghetti and milk, please," Jason replies.

Both Mom and Dad smile.

Clue for Christian Parents

Parents can develop a nonverbal vocabulary of positive reinforcement with a child. Smiles, winks, loving pats, etc. are a
part of this effective nonverbal language given for good
behavior. A child enjoys this "secret language" of communication and looks forward to each nonverbal sign of praise
and encouragement.

Wise parents will be ever on the alert to give such nonverbal
signs of love and affection. Sad to say, many a child seeks negative attention because it is the only attention that will be given.

The food arrives at the table. After the waitress is finished
serving the meal, Jason and his parents bow their heads,
close their eyes, and Dad thanks God for the food.

Clue for Christian Parents

It should be as natural for a family to thank God in a public
place for the food that he has provided as it is at home.
Such praise to God is a natural outgrowth of hearts that love
and serve a gracious God, who satisfies your desires with
good things so that your youth is renewed like the eagle's
(Psalm 103:5).

Jason, Mom, and Dad are enjoying a pleasant dinner.
When Jason reaches for a piece of bread, he fumbles and his
milk spills, going everywhere.

Humiliated and ready to cry, he looks at his parents, beginning to whimper, "I'm sorry. I didn't mean to—"

Mom grabs for the napkins and starts to blot up the mess. All
the while, she is telling her son, "It's OK, Jason. Don't worry."

"These things happen, Son," encourages Dad with a smile
and a loving arm around Jason. "Let's help Mom clean up."

After the milk is cleaned up and they settle down, Dad quips, "What is there about milk? Sometimes it just seems to jump out of the glass and go racing around. I've had it happen too, Jason . . . more times than I like to remember."

"Really, Dad? That makes me feel better." Jason sighs. "I'm sorry. I hope I won't do that again!"

"Your mom and I know that," Dad encourages. "Even with the spilled milk, Jason, you have been a wonderful boy tonight, and we are very proud of your behavior." He looks at his wife. "Well, honey, what do you think of our big boy?"

"I'm extremely proud of him, and so thankful that God gave him to us."

Clue for Christian Parents

Mistakes happen, no matter how hard a child tries. When a child is really trying to behave and a mistake happens, a parent has the God-given opportunity to lovingly affirm, help, and encourage the child. After all, as Christians, we are affirmed that God loves us unconditionally and handles our mistakes with unmerited mercy, gentleness, and loving-kindness. We must do the same for the children whom God entrusts to us.

Sitting near Jason and his parents is a family with three children who are somewhat out of control. The parents seem frazzled.

As Jason's family passes them to leave the restaurant, that dad smiles and says to Jason's dad, "It must be nice to have only one child."

Mom and Dad smile back, knowing that when they have more children they will continue to uphold godly principles in their home.

Clue for Christian Parents

It isn't the number of children in the home that makes the difference in discipline. It depends on the self-discipline of the parents to commit themselves to rearing each child "in the training and instruction of the Lord." This is true if a family has one child or one dozen.

In the car, Dad says, "Jason, it was a pleasure taking a big boy to dinner." He turns to his wife and squeezes her hand. "This was a good idea, dear. Let's do it again sometime! I've got an idea," he continues, winking at Jason. "Why don't we stop on the way home for an ice-cream cone?"

Jason grins. *"Awwwwllll riiiiiiiiight!"*

CONSISTENCY

The parent–child
power struggle unfolds
in the grocery store

The most important step in any disciplinary procedure is to establish reasonable expectations and boundaries in advance.

DR. JAMES DOBSON

Today I am giving you the choice between a blessing and a curse! You will be blessed if you obey the commands of the Lord your God that I am giving you today. You will receive a curse if you reject the commands of the Lord your God and turn from his way by worshiping foreign gods.

DEUTERONOMY 11:26-28

JASON IN CHARGE

Jason sometimes hears his mom listening to radio programs that say things like "If you're going to be a good parent, you've got to be consistent." Well, he figures his mom must be a good parent because she sure is consistent. She consistently lets him have anything he wants if he begs and pleads long enough!

Today they're going to the grocery store, and Jason is determined to get his mom to buy him the new Sugar Bits cereal that he's seen on TV. He can't wait to get the neat secret decoder ring that's inside!

Clue for Christian Parents

Jason is confident that he will reach his goal. From previous experience, he knows that even though his mom's first response may be negative, he will be able to wear her down with repeated asking in various ways.

29

"Mom, will you *please* buy me the new Sugar Bits cereal?"

Mom responds just like Jason knew she would. "No! It will rot your teeth and make you hyper!"

Clue for Christian Parents

So far, everything is going just as Jason knew it would. Unfortunately, Jason has learned that Mom's *nos* are not usually the final word. He now begins to whittle away at her patience.

As Jason and Mom enter the store, Jason whines, "I want to go home."

Jason's mom answers with loving patience. "We just got here, and you need to be good while Mommy's shopping."

"I'll be good if you buy me some Sugar Bits cereal."

"I told you *no,* and I meant it!" Jason's mom affirms.

Clue for Christian Parents

Mom is unaware that she is entering into an argument with her son. She does not realize that her first response should have been sufficient.

Two aisles over, Jason continues his barrage. "You're *soooooooo* mean! Johnny's mom bought him some!"

"Well, I'm not Johnny's mom!" she answers with all the authority she possesses.

Clue for Christian Parents

Jason's mom is clearly not in control of her child or the situation. At this point, she is beginning to worry about what other people in the store are thinking about her and about her son. She is right. Even the casual observer is wondering why this adult is allowing her child to control the situation.

Now they've arrived in the cereal aisle, and Jason throws his final punch. "I want it! I want it! *I want it now!*"

"You must stop that," the embarrassed mom hisses.

"People are looking. If you're a good boy for the rest of the shopping, we'll see."

Jason responds to his mother's direction by running down the aisles with a basket and bumping into people. Jason loves it. *Mom keeps telling me to stop, but I'm having too much fun!*

Clue for Christian Parents
Jason learned long ago that he doesn't have to obey his mom. His public, loud manipulation of his mother indicates his lack of respect for her authority. Already Jason has learned that verbal directions are meaningless and that boundaries are made to be crossed.

As they approach the checkout counter, Jason begins pleading, "Can we get it? Huh? Huh? Huh? Can we? Can we?"

"No, you have not been a good boy," his mom answers.

Clue for Christian Parents
Jason knows his mom better than his mom knows parenting. He knows that with one last maneuver, the cereal and decoder ring will be his. Jason has tested his mom and does not believe she really means no. Her no is merely an invitation to another parent-child struggle. To affirm leadership over his mother, Jason is bent on winning this battle.

At the checkout stand, Jason runs off, calling over his shoulder, "Mom, I'll be right back."

"Don't you go get that cereal. I said no!" Mom hollers after him.

A moment later, Jason reappears, Sugar Bits in hand.

"You take that back. I said no!" Mom insists.

"Oh, *pleeeeeease!*" Jason pleads with an adorable smile that lights up his face.

His mother's heart melts. "Oh, OK, but just this once."

Clue for Christian Parents

Jason and his mom will now leave the store amiably. Jason has gotten what he wanted, and his mom has a moment of peace—for a price!

Children must have choices and consequences. Jason was given neither. In this brief scenario, Mom had a choice to say what she meant and mean what she said—or to speak empty words. As a result of her choice to be manipulated and controlled by the whim of her child, the child's conception that he truly is in charge of himself and his mom was reinforced. Such responsibility is an absurd burden for any child to bear.

Q & A THAT LEAD THE WAY

Q: *What was Jason's objective?*

A: To get the secret decoder ring.

Q: *Did he meet his objective?*

A: Yes.

Q: *Was Mom consistent?*

A: Yes, but in the wrong way. Mom consistently gives in, and her words of authority mean nothing to her son. Jason has figured this out, but Mom hasn't. She still believes that she has control of her son's behavior. You can be certain that she could rationalize her behavior and her son's as soon as she left the parking lot.

Q: *What could Mom have done differently?*

A: Many things. This loving, well-meaning mom failed to establish reasonable expectations and boundaries. Jason needed to know that he was not going to get anything in the store. Or he needed to know that if he did not touch groceries or play with carts in the aisle, he could select something that both Jason and his mom had agreed upon in advance!

Every time you say no to your child without having set reasonable standards and expectations in advance, you must be prepared for a power struggle. You need to have a plan. Your child must know what is acceptable and what is not acceptable before being held responsible. Without a well-defined plan, what will you do when your child defies you with embarrassing vehemence in a public place or cajoles you with skillful manipulation?

Jason's mom had no plan. She had set no standards. There were no predetermined boundaries or expectations. She had not planned a consequence for bad behavior and communicated it to Jason. When a wrong choice is made, there needs to be a consequence. This well-meaning mom actually rewarded her son's defiance. Next time, Jason will be even stronger in his manipulation and defiance. Why? That's the way his mom is training him!

How does God discipline? All through his Word, he explains appropriate behavior. God sets boundaries. God establishes reasonable expectations. His people understand their responsibility. The consequences for both good choices and poor choices are given—over and over and over again! Then when a wrong choice is made—i.e., when we sin—the consequence must follow. Of course God still loves us. After all, "God showed his great love for us by sending Christ to die for us while we were still sinners" (Romans 5:8). But there is still a consequence for the poor choice. There is always a consequence for bad behavior.

34

That is how it must be in raising children. God has ordained parents to be in the position of authority over their children. There must always be a standard, and that standard needs to be verbalized before the activity begins. Then there must always be a consequence, and it needs to be verbalized to the child before the activity begins. You must clearly communicate boundaries and expectations. Your child must clearly understand his or her responsibility in each situation.

In this case, Mom needed to set the standards for behavior in the grocery store in advance. She also needed to let Jason know what would happen if he did not keep the standards. Then she needed to reemphasize the standards to Jason as a strong, single warning inside the store. After that, the choice to obey or disobey was his. The application of the consequence was the responsibility of the mother.

HOW TO REMOVE THE PARENT-CHILD POWER STRUGGLE IN THE GROCERY STORE

Well-defined boundaries give security. The parent, not the child, must set these boundaries. World-renowned family counselor and best-selling author Dr. James Dobson says, "The most important step in any disciplinary procedure is to establish reasonable expectations and boundaries in advance!" (*Temper Your Child's Tantrums*, Tyndale House, 1978, page 31).

Let's put this grocery store scenario into proper perspective. Whether you are just beginning to take your young child grocery shopping with you or you would like to change previously established behavior patterns, you need to set the boundaries before you leave the house.

MOM IN CHARGE

Mom takes some time before leaving the house to sit down with Jason and set the standards.

"Jason, please sit down. You and I are going to the grocery store today to get some things we need. What do you remember about going to the grocery store?"

Clue for Christian Parents

Why does Mom waste precious time asking questions? You *must* find out what your child is thinking and what your child's perceptions and expectations are. You may think you have communicated clearly and set definite boundaries, but you must make certain that your child understands. Listening to your child is the very best way to see if the standards are clear in the child's mind. If the child does not seem to understand, you can then clarify any misconceptions.

Even though you feel you don't have any time to waste, taking the time to sit down face-to-face with your child and set standards will definitely save you valuable time, energy, stress, and frustration. This is an imperative first step.

"Jason, at the grocery store there are many people and lots and lots of things to see and eat. Do you ever touch any of these things?"

Jason responds with understanding, "No!"

"That's right, not unless Mommy tells you to put something in the cart. Your hands are at your side or on the cart, and your feet are walking next to Mommy's at all times. Your voice will be a quiet voice that only Mommy can hear. What will happen if you obey Mommy the whole time we are in the store?"

Jason brightens. "You said I could pick the flavor of ice cream to bring home."

"That's right, dear. But what will happen if you don't obey Mommy in the grocery store?"

Jason answers, "I won't get to pick the ice cream, and I won't get to play when we get home."

Clue for Christian Parents

The giving of an appropriate reward is an encouragement to good behavior. The giving of a logical consequence for misbehavior strengthens the child's resolve to obey. God does it in his Word from Genesis to Revelation. Parents must also do this in each situation.

Mom asks one last question. "You may see other children in the store who are loud and not obedient. What will you do?"

Jason knows what is expected. "I will still obey you, Mom."

Mom explains further. "Even though everyone else may be doing the wrong thing, God wants us to obey and do what's right. You and I can be an example for other mothers and children by doing the right thing."

Clue for Christian Parents

Even a little child needs to learn to obey God no matter what others do. The child must also learn that when he or she chooses to obey, there is something far more important than a simple reward like choosing an ice-cream flavor. The child is obeying God and is showing others how God wants children to behave. The child is setting a godly example for others. Making the child aware of this "higher calling" sets a tone for the family that further removes the parent-child power struggle and replaces it with the team concept: Our family is a team working together to obey the Lord God Almighty and bring honor to his name.

"Now let's both ask God to help us to obey him and do what's right." Both Jason and Mom pray.

Clue for Christian Parents

There is power in prayer. From the time a child first learns to talk, that child can learn to talk to God. As Christian parents model praying throughout the day, the child will learn that praying is as natural a part of life as breathing. The child needs to hear Mom and Dad asking the Lord to help them to obey. The child needs to know that obedience is not easy for anyone of any age and that only with the help of the Holy Spirit is obedience possible.

In the car, Jason asks, "Mom, is Sugar Bits cereal on your list? Johnny showed me his cool secret decoder ring that's inside."

"Well, Jason, I have another cereal on the list, but I'll compare the price and ingredients, and we'll see."

Jason answers, "Thanks, Mom."

As they enter the store, Mom takes out the cart. Jason walks along, gaping at the wonders of the store. "Where should your hand be, Jason?" Mom reminds him. Jason quickly puts his hand on the cart, looks up at Mom, and says, "I'm sorry, Mom. I forgot."

Occasionally Mom asks Jason to get something from a bottom shelf and put it carefully in the cart. Jason obeys, and then holds onto the cart each time he finishes a task. Consistently, Mom smiles and voices approval. "Jason, you are doing a good job."

Clue for Christian Parents
When parents give positive reinforcement, children are encouraged to continue obeying. The consistent, earned praise Jason is receiving from his mother is rewarding his positive behavior. Jason knows his mother is aware of what is going on. She is looking for ways to give him deserved recognition.

In the cereal aisle, Mom is true to her word. She compares the Sugar Bits cereal to the one she has on her list. She decides that the sugar content is too high. She lets Jason know that although there is a great secret decoder ring in Sugar Bits, the cereal is too sugary, and she's decided not to buy it. Jason is disappointed, but he accepts her decision. He knows that his mother will *not* change her mind.

In the ice-cream aisle, Mom stops and lets Jason know she is very proud of his behavior in the store today. "Jason, you get to pick any flavor you want!" Eagerly, Jason looks over the choices. Mom can tell he's having a hard time making up his mind.

Clue for Christian Parents

Jason will not be allowed to select more than one flavor. He must learn to follow directions, even though this selection may be difficult for him to make. His mother said what she meant and meant what she said.

The wait at the checkout stand is long. The lady in line behind them remarks, "It must be nice to have such a big boy to help you with your shopping. It's too bad there aren't more children like your son."

Mom and Jason both look up and smile. "Yes," Mom replies, "he's been a great help."

In the car, Mom says, "You were a really big help shopping today, Jason. Thank you so very much. It's fun to have such a big boy helping me with the grocery shopping."

Jason beams from the backseat.

(Un)Common Courtesy

The inevitable and frequent parent–child telephone struggle

*Good parents are not afraid to be
momentarily disliked by children during
the act of enforcing rules.*

JEAN LAIRD

*If you refuse to discipline your children,
it proves you don't love them; if you love your children,
you will be prompt to discipline them.*

PROVERBS 13:24

JASON IN CHARGE

Jason is playing with his new train set. *This sure is fun!* he thinks. *It sounds just like a real train chugging along. I love the cool whistle—Hoooooot! Hooooooot! You can even change the sound and make it really soft or REALLLLLY LOUD! I like the loud sound best!*

The telephone rings. "Jason," Mom says clearly, "please turn your train off until I'm off the phone. Hello," Mom says into the phone. "Oh, hi, Sue. How are you?"

Jason frowns. *Oh, no!* he says to himself. *It's Mom's best friend. She'll probably be on the phone forever!*

All too soon, Jason becomes impatient. *I'm not having fun!* he realizes. *I don't think Mom will notice if I turn the train on and use the soft sound.* Jason looks toward his mom and turns the volume on softly.

Jason's mom notices that the train is back on but thinks, *Well, at least he's got the volume down.*

Clue for Christian Parents

Every child deserves to have a parent who loves him enough to say what is meant and to mean what is said! Anything less shows a lack of respect for the child and for oneself.

Jason's mom ignored his disobedience. By allowing him to turn the train back on without even recognizing his willfulness and with no consequence for wrongdoing, she sends a clear message to Jason: *Jason, you do not have to obey me.*

Clearly, there is a lack of mutual respect. John Rosemond, author of the newspaper column "Parent to Parent," states: "Children demonstrate respect for their parents by calmly obeying them. Parents demonstrate respect for their children by calmly expecting them to obey."

Moments later, Jason laments, *I'm not having that much fun with the volume down. Mom's been on the phone too long, anyway. I think I'll crank it up.*

As the noise becomes louder and louder, Jason can see his mom turn around and put her "shush finger" to her mouth, giving him an angry look.

Jason looks at his mom and then goes back to his train. He thinks, *I know Mom hates to interrupt the person on the phone. I'll just keep on playing. Then maybe she'll get off sooner.*

44

Clue for Christian Parents

Jason knows from past experience that Mom will not interrupt her phone conversation to discipline him. At this point, Jason is actually beginning to discipline his mom. She's been on the phone too long, and he wants her off. Consciously or unconsciously, he knows that if he escalates his disobedience, he will get his way. His mom will have to get off the phone.

Jason becomes louder with his play. "ALL ABOARD!" Jason yells. Mom frowns severely and gives Jason a more energetic shush signal. Jason continues his loud play. Mom begins to talk louder to her friend in order to be heard over Jason's play.

At this point, Jason leaves his train running and goes over to his mom. Without any hesitation, he demands, "I'm hungry. I want lunch!"

"Excuse me, Sue," Mom says politely. Putting her hand over the mouthpiece, she says sternly, "We'll have lunch in a little while," and goes back to her conversation.

"I'm hungry *now!*" Jason yells.

Jason's mom is embarrassed that her friend Sue has heard Jason's outburst and tries to politely end the conversation rather than discipline her son on the spot.

Clue for Christian Parents

Jason has no clue as to what "a little while" means. All he knows is that his mom's friend is taking too much of her time, he is supposed to be quiet for too long, and it doesn't seem like it will ever end!

Jason's mom feels torn between the friend on the phone and her son. Neither is getting her full attention, and she seems incapable of controlling her son's behavior. Getting off the phone quickly doesn't seem to be an option either.

There are several ways Jason's mom could have avoided this problem. For one thing, Jason needed to know exactly how he was required to behave when his mom was on the phone. He also needed to know what the consequences of any misbehavior would be. These standards needed to be established long before the telephone rang.

It also would have been considerate for Jason's mom to have given him a time frame for the telephone conversation. For example, "I'll be on the phone until the big hand points to the four" or "I'll be on the phone until this timer goes off." Then Jason would have had some tangible way of anticipating the conversation ending, something he could comprehend.

Another option would have been for Jason's mom to politely tell her friend, "I can't give you the time you deserve right now. Would it be convenient for you if I call you back at (such and such a time)?"

Then the friend who needed to talk would not have been offended by the lack of attention, and both Jason and his mom would have saved face.

Jason is becoming more and more impatient. *If she's not going to get me lunch, I'll just get it myself.*

Jason goes over to the refrigerator and opens the door. He swings from the door as he tries to see what he can eat. Eggs

are falling out of the door and onto the floor. "Wow! This is cool!" Jason exclaims.

Mom looks over at the mess she's going to have to clean up. Sue is almost finished talking. Mom says, "I'd better go now. I'll talk to you later."

As the phone clicks off, Jason's mom screams, "Jason! Mommy was trying to talk on the phone!"

"But I'm hungry, and you were on the phone a really loooooong time," Jason says sweetly.

Guilt sets in as Mom realizes that she has been on the phone a lot with Sue lately because of her friend's marital problems. "I'm sorry, honey. What do you want for lunch? I'll fix it right after I get these eggs cleaned up."

Q & A THAT LEAD THE WAY

Q: *If you ask a child to wait, should you expect that child to wait?*

A: Absolutely. Teaching a child to wait patiently is essential. *However,* the period of time that you ask a child to wait

47

must be appropriate to the age and stage of the child's development.

How can you know what is appropriate? As Christian parents, we have a tremendous advantage. We can approach God's throne of grace in prayer at any time of the day or night and ask for wisdom and discernment concerning our children. As we diligently pray, search God's Word, become keen observers of our children, and read and ask questions of godly parenting authorities, God will lead us into making the right decisions to mold the hearts of our children and to develop godly character in them.

Q: *How can a parent strike a balance between being there for a friend who needs help and paying attention to her child?*

A: Friends have problems and sometimes need us. Because we care, we want to give them our time and attention. However, our own families are our first responsibility. That includes disciplining and building character in our children.

Although we want to be available to meet the needs of our friends, particularly during times of crisis, we must remember that our children also deserve uninterrupted time. Giving them 100 percent of our attention at certain times assures them of our love, interest, and respect. At these special times, the answering machine can take the messages.

Letting the child know "You and I are going to play/talk/read together for the next fifteen minutes no matter how often the phone rings" is a real encouragement to a child. Children deserve our time and full attention for certain segments of each day. Parents who plan for these times are delighted with the results!

Q: *Was it a good idea for Mom to give the shush sign to Jason when she was on the phone?*

A: Oh, yes. There are many instances where it is not only advisable but necessary to use nonverbal warnings with our children. A child must be trained to understand what these nonverbal signs mean. Even more important than understanding the meaning of the nonverbal sign, however, the child must understand that a choice to disobey the warning will lead to an appropriate consequence.

Q: *What could Mom have done differently when Jason demanded lunch?*

A: Because Jason's mom did not establish reasonable standards for behavior while she was on the telephone or set a reasonable length of time for Jason to wait patiently, she set herself up for what happened.

In spite of these omissions, it would have been helpful if Jason's mom had had a more significant, preestablished nonverbal gesture to use when Jason ignored her shush sign. For example, snapping fingers and pointing to the child's room is a highly appropriate signal that can mean "Remove yourself from the telephone area *now* and take time out in your room until Mom is available to come and handle the infraction."

Since Jason's mom did not have such a plan in place, however, she needed to end her conversation with Sue and deal with Jason's compounded disobedience. Although her friend needed counseling and a sympathetic ear, her son needed to develop the godly character qualities of obedience, respect, patience, self-control, responsibility, and kindness. That was the more urgent and the more important job for Jason's mom at that moment.

Q: *If your child is disobedient and then compounds the disobedience by willfully and deliberately making a mess, who is responsible to clean it up?*

A: The child! If the mess is greater than the child's ability to clean it up, the child must still be required to spend a significant amount of time attempting to clean it up—without your help! You must not rescue children from the natural consequences of their own rebellion. This important principle is clearly taught in God's Word. God loves unconditionally, but the consequences of willful rebellion still go into effect.

Q: *Should Jason's mom have felt guilty?*

A: Yes, because she *was* guilty—guilty of poor parenting. She did not plan ahead so that Jason, her friend, and she herself all understood the time constraints.

Variations of this type of situation are typical for all parents. This kind of "good guilt" is what causes us to humble ourselves before the Lord, confess our sins, and ask for his wisdom and guidance.

Actually, with the right kind of response on your part, this kind of situation can provide the threshold of a whole new beginning for you and your child.

Jason's mom attempted to remove her guilt by ignoring and excusing her son's disobedient rebellion. It would have been far wiser to have taken these five simple steps:

1. Apologize to her son for the way she handled the telephone call.
2. With her son at her side listening, confess the problem to God and ask for direction and wisdom.
3. Have her son talk to God, confess his sin of willful disobedience, and ask the Lord to cleanse him and help him be obedient, patient, respectful, kind, and responsible in the future.
4. Set reasonable expectations for the next time Mom is on the phone and give consequences for disobedience.
5. Have her son clean up as much of the mess as he can without her help.

How to Remove the Parent-Child Telephone Struggle

Let's demonstrate how Mom could have taken control of this all-too-common situation.

Mom in Charge

"Jason, you and I need to have a talk. Please come here and sit down. Who has Mommy been spending a lot of time talking to on the phone lately?"

Jason answers without hesitation, "Grandma, Aunt Suzie, Aunt Rachel, Daddy sometimes, and some other people, but I don't know their names."

Clue for Christian Parents

Once again, a smart mom will ask her child questions so she can understand the child's perceptions and thoughts. It is vitally important to know what the child is thinking in order to know what to say to the child and how to say it effectively. Using the "meeting" approach, Mom is establishing the importance of the topic to be discussed. If your child has already learned that while you are on the telephone, you tend to overlook disobedience, invest the time to sit down with your child, set reasonable standards, and establish appropriate consequences. This investment will pay *big* dividends in future peace and contentment in the home! Even more important, the character of the child is being molded in a God-honoring way.

"Do you remember Mommy's friend Sue?"

Jason nods.

"Well, Jason, she has some problems, so Mommy needs to listen to her on the phone, talk to her, and pray with her. Do you think it is a good thing to help a friend?"

Jason replies immediately, "Sure, Mom."

"I need your help, too, Jason, while I am on the telephone. How do you think you can help?"

Jason is thoughtful. "Do you want me to listen and talk and pray with you on the phone?"

Mom smiles gently and gives her son a hug. "That's a good idea, dear, and you and I will certainly want to pray together for Sue, but today Sue and I need to talk alone on the phone. How will you help so Mommy can listen to Sue and talk to her and pray with her?"

Clue for Christian Parents

A wise parent affirms a child not only by asking questions but by listening to the child's answers with full attention. Whenever possible, you need to indicate that your child's answers are good, even though they may not be exactly what you were looking for.

Jason's mom is also including him in the plans. She is wise enough to know that for her to give her friend her full attention, Jason will need to be quiet and occupied. She also realizes that, as a functioning member of the family, he deserves to know why it is important for him to be respectful, especially since this may be an unusually long conversation and difficult to break off after it's started.

Jason responds, "I can play quietly with my train."

His mother hesitates. "Isn't it a little hard to play with your train without turning it on and making sounds?"

"Yes, I guess so, Mom, but I could try."

"Thank you, Jason, for being willing to try, but that might be just too hard. What else could you do?"

Clue for Christian Parents

Ideally, a parent should never put a young child in a situation knowing it is going to be impossible for the child to obey. That sets the child up for failure, and that is wrong. God never asks his children to do more than they are capable of doing with his strength, wisdom, and guidance. We must model God's example with the children God has given us.

Jason thinks hard, then brightens. "I can look at my books."

"Great idea, Jason, and you have so many wonderful books. But if you want to do something else while I am on the phone, you may also play quietly with your blocks, do puzzles, or color."

Clue for Christian Parents

A wise parent overplans. All too often a serious phone conversation goes on *much* longer than expected. A child needs to have many choices available.

"Jason, I need to ask you an important question. When I am on the telephone talking to Sue, will you try to talk to me?"

Jason drops his head and shakes it. "No, Mom, I'll try not to."

"Thank you, Jason. It is very important that you try not to talk to me while I am talking to Sue on the telephone. This is my time for Sue, not for you. I know that you have been having a little trouble in this area of obedience. Just in case this should happen today, I want to remind you that you will hear me snap my fingers. What will that mean?"

"It means that you want me to stop right now and look at you," Jason correctly recalls.

"That's right, Jason. Then, if it should happen again, which I'm certain it won't, I will need to not only snap my fingers but also point to your room. What will that mean?"

Jason answers thoughtfully, "That means I need to go to my room and have time-out until you come."

Clue for Christian Parents

Your child's continual interrupting while you are on the phone shouts out the message: *I have no control of my child, and my child has no respect for me or for anybody else!*

Naturally, almost every child will try to interrupt when a parent is on the phone. If this interrupting behavior is allowed, it will continue and become an ingrained habit. This rude and selfish behavior will stop if you train your child by establishing and following through on appropriate consequences that the child knows and understands.

"And if you should have to go to your room for time-out, what will that mean, Jason?"

Jason sadly replies, "It means I have to just sit there and do nothing except think about what I did wrong and what I need to do next time."

"You are so right, Jason! I certainly hope that will not happen!"

"Me, too, Mom!"

Clue for Christian Parents

Time-out should not be fun! Too often parents say that their children do not mind having time-outs in their rooms because there's so much to do! That approach will not correct wrong behavior.

Time-out needs to be a disciplinary action, a no-fun consequence. A child who is sent to his or her room for time-out needs to be required to sit in the middle of the floor, touching nothing. (If the child does not follow this established guideline, appropriate consequences must follow!) The child must spend this time contemplating the act of disobedience and thinking about what needs to be done differently in the future.

When you come into the room, have your child verbalize what the wrongdoing was, what should have been done, and what will be done next time. Together, the two of you

need to talk to the Lord. Your child needs to confess the disobedience to the Lord, ask for forgiveness, and ask the Lord
for help in doing the right thing in the future. You need to
thank the Lord for his great love for your child that sent
Jesus to die on the cross for that child's mistakes, thank the
Lord for giving this child to you, and ask the Lord to help
you be the kind of parent who will please the Lord.

Such a disciplinary session provides an extremely positive
opportunity to teach your child about the love, forgiveness,
and mercy of God and to reassure your child of his or her
innate worth as a person created in the image of God.

It also provides the opportunity to reassure your child of
your own love and care. Your child needs to know that making mistakes is normal because nobody is perfect and that
you love, value, and appreciate him or her in spite of mistakes. Your child also needs to know that your love is so
great that you will never ignore wrongdoing but will deal
with it in a fair, appropriate manner.

"There is only one other thing we need to discuss, Jason,"
Mom says.

"What's that, Mom?" Jason wonders.

"I may need to be on the phone for at least twenty or
thirty minutes, so I will set the timer and put it on the shelf
where you and I will both be able to see it. I just want you to
know that when the timer goes off, I will say good-bye to
Sue, get off the phone, and fix your lunch. Do you understand?"

Jason seems relieved. "Thanks, Mom. I'm already starting
to get a little hungry."

Clue for Christian Parents
Telephone conversations almost always seem to last too
long for a young child. A wise parent will recognize this
and set limits, not only for the child's behavior and activities

but also for the length of time she will be on the telephone.

A timer is an extremely useful tool in child rearing. The timer gives the child the hope and assurance that there will be an end to the conversation. The timer also teaches the child the concept of time passing.

"Jason, it's almost time for me to call Sue. She is waiting for my call. What would be a good thing for you and me to do before I call?" Jason looks blank. "You had such a good idea. You suggested that we pray for Sue together. Do you remember?"

Jason beams. "I do now, Mom!" Jason and his mom bow their heads together and pray for Sue and the conversation and for Jason's behavior while they are on the phone.

Clue for Christian Parents

Whenever possible, a wise parent will plan with the child for the more lengthy phone call, realizing how difficult it is for the young child to keep appropriately occupied for the entire time.

It is extremely advantageous for the mom of the younger child/children to be the one to make the call or to arrange for the caller to call at a designated time. This really helps in the planning. It is also important to share the time limit of the call with the other person so that everyone involved knows the plan.

Jason's mom feels confident that Jason knows and understands the standards. Jason watches while she sets the timer and puts it in place. She watches while he gets himself occupied and compliments him.

Then she makes the call to Sue.

All goes well for the first few minutes. Then Jason peeks at his mom. In his hand is a picture that he has drawn. He comes closer and holds it up. His mom snaps her fingers. Jason retreats for a time.

After a few more minutes Jason comes up behind Mom, touching her and preparing to give a hug. He holds up the picture and opens his mouth to whisper. His mom snaps her fingers again and points to his bedroom.

A very sad and disappointed Jason heads for the bedroom with the picture drooping alongside.

The timer goes off. Mom gets off the phone and comes to the bedroom. She has a very serious look on her face.

Before Mom says a word, Jason apologizes. "I'm sorry, Mom. I just wanted to show you the great picture I drew."

"Jason, you know I like to see your drawings," Mom says. "But was that the time to show me your drawing?"

Jason shakes his head.

"Was that the time to try to hug me or to whisper?"

Jason shakes his downcast head again.

"What *should* you have done, Jason?" Mom asks.

Jason repeats the standards that were set ahead of time.

"Why did I need to snap my fingers twice and send you to your room?"

Jason remembers—all too well!

Clue for Christian Parents
As Christian parents who desire to build godly character into our children, it is crucial that we require our children to accept responsibility for their actions, even at an early age.

After the misbehavior, your questions lead the way for your child to accept ownership of the disobedience and responsibility for the consequence.

"What do we need to do now, Jason?" Mom asks.

Jason has been through this many times before. He is able to verbalize the steps. "I need to tell you what I did wrong, tell you I'm sorry, and ask you to forgive me. Then I need to pray and tell God what I did wrong, ask him for forgiveness, and ask him to help me do the right thing next time."

Jason and his mom do this together.

Clue for Christian Parents

The wise parent diligently trains the child in dealing with wrongdoing, so that even a young child is able to verbalize the steps that lead from the disobedience to confession to repentance and into forgiveness with you and with the Lord. If another person is involved in the disobedience, that person must also be a part of the confession, repentance, and forgiveness process.

Being forgiven is glorious! After the consequence of wrongdoing has been administered and the child has been forgiven, the young child's life is given a fresh start, a new beginning. It is a privilege for a parent to be a part of this character-building process. Yes, it seems to take such a *long* time when time is always short. Yet the sacrifice of a relatively few minutes bears spiritual fruit for time and eternity in the life of your child.

"Are you ready for lunch, Jason?"

Jason smiles broadly. "I sure am, Mom!"

"Me, too, Jason! You may have either a tuna sandwich or a peanut-butter-and-jelly sandwich. Which would you like?"

"I'd like peanut butter 'n' jelly, please!"

Mom smiles. "Good choice. I think that's what I'll have, too." They hold hands and head for the kitchen.

NONVERBAL COMMUNICATION

The parent–child
power struggle continues
when friends come to visit

The thing that impresses me most about America is the way parents obey their children.

THE DUKE OF WINDSOR

Children, obey your parents because you belong to the Lord, for this is the right thing to do.

EPHESIANS 6:1

JASON IN CHARGE

Mom has invited a new friend who has a son about Jason's age over for lunch. Mom has decided not to tell Jason about it yet because she doesn't want to take the time to answer such questions as "Why are they coming over?" "Who are they?" "What does the boy look like?" etc. It is more important to her to get her house in tip-top shape. After all, her new friend has never seen her home.

"Jason, go play outside until I'm finished cleaning," she tells Jason. "This place is a filthy pigpen."

"It doesn't look any different than it always does," Jason grumbles on his way outside.

Clue for Christian Parents

No wonder Jason has no interest in the housecleaning. He's not involved. It has nothing to do with him. Why should he care? It's only taking away from his time with Mom and from doing what he wants to do. A family is a team, and part of the teamwork needs to include cleaning.

"Mom's been cleaning the house for too long," Jason declares after a few minutes. "I wonder why. I'm getting bored. I'm tired of playing outside. I guess I'll go in, but I sure hope she turns off the vacuum soon. I just hate the sound of that thing. I know—I'll ask her if we can go to the park!"

Clue for Christian Parents
Jason does not hesitate to disobey his mother's instructions when they are no longer easy for him to obey. Why should he be concerned about disobedience? Past experience has shown him that his mom only means what she says for a little while or until Jason chooses not to comply for his own reason.

"Hi, Jason! Mommy is having a friend over for lunch today. She has a little boy about your age, and I want you to share your toys and play nicely while we are talking."

"But I wanted to go to the park."

Clue for Christian Parents
Everyone likes to know what's going on, especially when the plan directly concerns them. So do children. Both children and adults need the opportunity to organize their thinking by knowing what's expected of them in advance. Jason was not included in the planning or told why his mom was cleaning or what the plans for the day were.

"No, we can't go to the park today. We don't have time. We have friends coming over. We can go to the park another day."

"But I want to go to the park, and besides—*I* don't have a friend coming over. I don't even know this kid."

64

Clue for Christian Parents

Mom's lack of preplanning is now affecting her child's attitude. Jason didn't know what was going to happen. He had an idea of his own. Now he's being told that his plan won't work, and he doesn't like it.

"I'm sure you will like him. He's a very nice boy. Go get a clean shirt on and comb your hair."

Clue for Christian Parents

Jason's mom is very conscious of her time problem. The guests are due to arrive. So she changes the subject and gives a new directive. Unfortunately, the situation involving the park has not been resolved. Jason's disobedience in coming into the house was totally ignored.

"No! There's nothing wrong with this shirt. I want to wear it."

"You do as I say, young man."

Clue for Christian Parents

Unwittingly, Jason's mom has just entered a power struggle with her son. She is frustrated and has no idea how this happened or what is causing her son to be defiant. Mom simply does not understand that Jason is using her lack of preparation and planning with him against her. He is also well aware of her repeated lack of follow-through after giving instructions.

Jason scowls at his mom and kicks the wall as he goes off down the hall to his room.

Clue for Christian Parents
Poor body language and an inappropriate show of anger should have an immediate and appropriate consequence. Scowling and kicking the wall show a lack of respect for Mom. Respect is a crucial part of good discipline.

Alone in his room, Jason grumbles, "She can't tell me what to wear." He gets an idea: *I'll just stay in here until the lady comes. Mom won't say anything about my shirt in front of her friend!*

Clue for Christian Parents
Jason is confident that his mom will get busy and not check up to see if he has done what he was told to do. If he just stays out of her sight for a little while, he can get by with the disobedience.

In a short time, Jason hears the doorbell and comes out of his room. "Jason," Mom says as she turns to look at him. She notices the shirt and the uncombed hair and frowns at Jason.

"Hey, Mom! That kid's shirt is dirty, too!"

Jason's mom is obviously embarrassed. She turns to her friend with a forced smile. "Kids do say the darnedest things. What's a mother to do?"

Clue for Christian Parents
Jason certainly has the upper hand in this situation. Mom's excuse and denial reaffirmed her helpless state to her son, to her friend, and to her friend's son. Now she will once again ignore his behavior and try to move forward with her plan for the afternoon.

"Jason, this is Timmy. Why don't you take him into your room to play while his mom and I talk."

"Naw, I want to watch TV in the family room," Jason says.

"We're going to be visiting in the family room, so you need to play in your room," Mom says firmly.

Clue for Christian Parents
Jason has learned from previous experience that if he really wants to watch television he can just go over and turn it on. He knows his mom will not want to argue with him in front of guests, so she'll just go into another room to talk rather than have a confrontation.

Jason's mom comes up with an idea before her son defies her. "Maybe you can play with your new cars."

"Oh, all right, come on," Jason says with a noticeably bad attitude.

Jason's mom is relieved that her suggestion worked and sits down to talk with her new friend.

All too soon, Jason's mom hears Jason yelling in his room. She rushes in to see Jason pulling a car from Timmy's hands. "Mom!" he shrieks, "Timmy's got my favorite car!"

Jason's mom admonishes, "Jason, remember we talked about sharing?"

Looking at Timmy's mom, she excuses Jason's behavior by saying, "He's probably tired." To Jason she says, "You sound like you must be hungry. Let's have lunch!"

Clue for Christian Parents

Making excuses for a child's behavior teaches the child to do the same. It does not take a child long to become a master at playing the "blame game" when parents model the technique.

Refusing to accept personal responsibility for words and actions is the essence of the blame game being played by people of all ages across America today. Everybody's got an excuse! All too soon, this child will be telling his teacher, his principal, his probation officer, "It isn't really my fault. I did it because . . ."

Curiously enough, Adam and Eve were the first to play this game. Adam blamed Eve, and Eve blamed the serpent. God was not impressed. They were still held accountable for their behavior, and the consequences rolled into action.

Parents have a responsibility to be accountable to God for their behavior—without excuse. Children must learn to be accountable to God and to their parents for their behavior—without excuse. They must also learn to be responsible for the consequences of their behavior.

During lunch, Mom keeps frowning at Jason; finally, she tells him to sit still and stop interrupting. This happens again and again.

Lunch ends abruptly when Jason, waving his arms, knocks over his full glass of milk. It drenches Timmy's unfinished meal as well as his own, splatters over the table, and drizzles onto the floor.

"Boys will be boys," Mom laughs nervously.

Clue for Christian Parents

Once again, Jason's mom is playing the blame game brilliantly. There is always an excuse for Jason's misbehavior. If this pattern continues, she will have the opportunity to continue to excuse his irresponsible behavior and her irresponsible parenting to many people—parents, coaches, and authority figures of all kinds.

Parents who have raised boys "with the discipline and instruction approved by the Lord" (Ephesians 6:4) don't buy it when a helpless mom defends her parenting problems with a shrug and "it's because he's a boy!" Nonsense!

Scripture makes no such distinction. The Word of God, our ultimate source of truth, states simply and clearly in Ephesians 6:1, "Children, obey your parents . . . for this is the right thing to do."

Many other directives to parents are just as clear and specific. For example, Proverbs 22:6 promises, "Teach your children to choose the right path, and when they are older, they will remain upon it."

This Scripture is not only an encouragement but also a solemn warning. If a parent trains a child to play the blame game, to make excuses rather than be accountable and responsible for his or her actions, the child will remain on that path. "When they are older, they will remain upon it." *Gulp!*

Timmy's mom makes an excuse about having to run some errands. They leave immediately.

Mom is very upset with Jason after they leave. She yells, "Jason, you were awful! Go to your room and stay there!"

Sullenly Jason goes off to his room.

Clue for Christian Parents

Notice that Jason's mom does not ask Jason about his behavior, nor does she review the standards of behavior that were set and not met. But then, she couldn't do that, since she failed to set clear limits or boundaries. Jason was not told what behavior was expected or what the consequences would be for misbehavior, nor was he encouraged with a positive reward if he chose to obey.

Soon Jason grows tired of playing with his army men, comes out of his room, and turns on cartoons.

Mom is in the kitchen washing up the lunch dishes. She notices that Jason has disobeyed her instruction to stay in his room. *Well, at least he's being quiet,* she muses. *I didn't even get to talk with my friend. Next time I'll get a sitter, and we'll go out to lunch.*

Clue for Christian Parents

For the sake of momentary peace in the house, Jason's mom has chosen—once again—to ignore her son's disobedience. That unfortunate choice perpetuates and strengthens Jason's role as the controlling authority figure in the family.

Because this mom did not deal with the misbehavior, she has lost the opportunity to affirm the importance of behavioral standards for a Christian family as a way of honoring the Lord. Jason has not been able to tell his mom what he should have done and what he knows he must do next time. He has not had the privilege of seeking forgiveness from God and from his mom for his behavior or the joy of being forgiven by God and his mom as a result of his prayer-

70

ful repentance. Neither he nor his mom has experienced the strengthening of their relationship with one another and with the Lord as a result of being cleansed and forgiven.

Jason has also lost the opportunity to build godly character that comes from admitting a mistake, assuming the responsibility for the mistake, and accepting the negative consequence for the behavior.

Q & A THAT LEAD THE WAY

Q: *Should Jason have been included in the cleaning?*

A: Yes! He needed to feel he was part of the team. Of course it is often more of a "pain" than a "gain" to have a little one help in the cleaning. He didn't need to help for a long time. Just a few moments would have assured him that he was part of the preparation process.

Q: *Is it really necessary to tell a child what the plans are?*

A: Absolutely, especially if the child is part of the plan. In this case, Jason was a large part of the plan, and he was the last to know. Neither children nor adults appreciate feeling left out of the planning.

Q: *Is it ever appropriate for a child to say no to a parent when asked to do something?*

A: No. When you ask your child to do something, the child should obey immediately, the first time the request is given. However, the request must be appropriate and not stir up an unnecessary power struggle.

In this case, by the time Jason's mom told him to change his shirt, she had unwittingly set up a power struggle. Jason did not know what the plans were (i.e., a mom and son were coming over), was not included in the preparation (i.e., the cleaning of the house), and was told the plan for the day only after being told that his idea wouldn't work (i.e., going to the park).

Q: *Even though Jason's mom could have handled the initial situation better, should she have ignored Jason's behavior when the guests were in their home?*

A: Absolutely not! The ancient saying "Two wrongs don't make a right" can certainly apply in this situation.

Ignoring wrong behavior in a child is inexcusable. Each time you ignore wrong behavior, you are really ignoring your child's cry for discipline! Each time you ignore wrong behavior, you miss an opportunity to develop godly character in your child. Each time you ignore wrong behavior, you are encouraging rebellious and defiant behavior toward authority.

Q: *Because the mom was in such a difficult situation, was it OK to excuse Jason's behavior? After all, she was the one who created it.*

A: No! Too many insecure and frustrated parents are eager to take the blame for their child's behavior or to give the child an excuse. These children grow up finding excuses for problems instead of learning to solve them.

Q: *Isn't yelling or screaming at a child a typical reaction to frustration?*

A: Certainly. But it does not make it right. Screaming lets the child (and anyone else within earshot) know that the authority figure has lost control. Jason's mom has plenty of reason to scream. She has mishandled the day and has suffered the embarrassing consequences. Her friend has seen her as a poor hostess and an ineffectual parent. Her son has also seen her as a very weak authority figure.

Jason chose to obey his mom when she screamed because it suited him for the moment. When he didn't want to stay in his room any longer, he came out, having no concern for consequences, and—of course—there weren't any (once again!).

Q: *Do you blame the mom for wanting to get a sitter next time and go out for lunch?*

A: No! What mom would want to repeat that sad experience? No one likes to be embarrassed; to be humiliated in your own home by your own child is a disgrace.

Jason's mom needed to establish reasonable expectations—in advance. Jason needed to know the boundaries for his behavior—in advance. Both of them needed to know the consequences—in advance. Both needed to decide what the negative consequence of misbehavior would be and what the positive rewards for acceptable behavior would be.

If this mom had been wise enough to take the time to think and prayerfully plan the day, she would have saved herself embarrassment and frustration and would have built character into the child God gave to her.

HOW TO REMOVE THE PARENT-CHILD POWER STRUGGLE WHEN FRIENDS COME TO VISIT

Many children experience anxiety when new people come to their home. It is always a good idea to set children down before guests arrive and let them know who's coming over, why they're coming over, how long they'll be there, and what is expected of the children.

Almost always, a certain amount of preparation is necessary before guests come for a visit in the home. Prayerful advance planning is the key. The parent who takes the time to think and pray through each situation will avoid the familiar pitfalls that annoy, discourage, and dishearten.

Let's rework this scenario with Mom in charge as she should be.

MOM IN CHARGE

Mom and Jason are sitting together at the breakfast table. Mom asks, "Do you remember when I told you last night at dinner that we are having two people over for lunch?" Jason nods.

Clue for Christian Parents

This smart mom has created a *we-not-me* situation. Notice that in reviewing the plans for the day, she reminds Jason that *they* are having guests. She has included Jason. He's an important part of this plan, and he knows it.

"I told you their names and some other things about them. What do you remember?"

Jason recalls several specifics.

"What a good listener you were, Jason!"

Clue for Christian Parents

This wise mom did not spring this situation on her son but provided ample time for him to get used to the idea. Asking questions about the coming event (whatever it may be) after a few hours is an excellent way to determine how clear the communication has been and just exactly what your child's perceptions may be. Then you will know if further explanation or clarification is needed.

"Jason, look around the house. What do you think we need to do before Timmy and his mommy come?"

Jason can't think of a thing.

Clue for Christian Parents

Children often resent the cleaning and cooking time that moms need to prepare for guests because it takes their mom's time and attention away from them. To avoid this resentment, a wise mom will train the child to "see" what needs to be done to provide an acceptable entertaining environment (without overdoing it, please!) This is part of training a child to know how to be a gracious host. Sad to say, many children are deprived of this opportunity and become adults who lack skills in this area.

Jason and his mom establish that some cleaning/straightening up/cooking preparations are required before the guests arrive. "While you put away the toys, Jason, I will vacuum. Let me know when you are finished, and I will come and check your work."

Jason is "finished" in very little time and comes to his mom. His mom checks. "Jason, you have done a very good job putting away the animals and the cars. Now you need to put away all the Lego pieces in the box and get the puzzle pieces that are still under the bed and put them in their place. I'll do some more vacuuming. Let me know when you are finished, and I'll check again."

Clue for Christian Parents

This mom follows through quickly. A young child needs immediate reinforcement. Although Jason had more to do, his mom was eager to find where her son had earned praise for being obedient and following directions. Had the mom only pointed out what her son had *not* done, Jason would have been discouraged from continuing on with his assignment.

As parents we must be on the alert to give our children justified praise, no matter how small the accomplishment. Our heavenly Father is gracious and loving to us and ever encouraging. The Lord never blasts us away with all our omissions. We could not bear it. So it must be when we deal with our children.

Jason again comes to Mom in a short period of time. Mom stops her vacuuming, goes to Jason's room, and checks. "Jason, you have done a good job putting away the Lego pieces. There were a *lot* of them to put away." Jason smiles and agrees. Mom notices that some of the puzzle pieces are still under the bed.

"Jason, you've put away most of the puzzle pieces, but can you see some that are still under the bed?" Jason wishes they weren't there, but he does see them when Mom points them out. Mom can tell that Jason's cleaning attention span is nearly spent!

"You've worked hard, Jason. Let me help you now. Let's pick up the rest of the puzzle pieces together and put them away." Jason is visibly relieved and quickly crawls under the bed to get the remaining pieces as Mom assists. The job is completed in seconds.

"Hooray, Jason! We're done! Thank you for doing such a good job." Mom gives Jason a deserved hug. Jason is obviously delighted with the hug—and that the task is completed!

Clue for Christian Parents

A parent must be very patient as the young child learns to straighten up a room. Although even young children are capable of doing a certain amount alone for a minimal amount of time, they need a *huge* amount of positive encouragement. Of course it would take far less time for a busy mom to do it herself. It's much more time consuming to tell a child what to do, begin vacuuming (or whatever), then be interrupted in less than two minutes, go with the child, check, praise, give suggestions, and then repeat the whole thing two minutes later. (And then end up doing most of it herself, anyway!)

But remember: "Don't get tired of doing what is good. Don't get discouraged and give up" (Galatians 6:9). You are *training* your child. Yes, it's a tough job, but somebody's got to do it—and God has ordained that somebody is *you!*

The good news is that if you train your child to help around the house when the child is young and impressionable, you will be blessed in later years by a child who not only knows what to do but will also know how to do it. In this case, the parent is instilling the value of household work—the need for the work, the way to work, and the fulfillment of a job well done.

The sensitive parent is also keenly aware of the child's limitations. This sensitive mom realized she could not press Jason any further with requests and suggestions. He was reaching his limit. Did she give up her directions? No way! She merely lent a hand so the task was still completed as requested. She also modeled being a team player in getting Jason's room ready.

"Jason, thank you so very much for putting your toys away. Please come here." Jason sits down and looks at his mother. She makes direct eye contact and says, "When our guests arrive, I will introduce you to Mrs. Johnson and her son, Timmy. Remember to look right at them and say, 'It's nice to meet you.' Then you can show Timmy to your room and ask him what he wants to play with. Why will you ask Timmy what he wants to do?"

Jason responds, "Because he's a guest, Mom."

"Good for you, Jason! You are right! But what will you do if he wants to do something you would rather not do?"

Jason looks puzzled. "How about if I tell him to play something else?"

Mom gently asks, "Is that the kind way to treat a guest?"

Jason shakes his head. "I guess not. I'll just do what he wants."

Mom gives her son a hug. "Now that is being a very kind boy, the way Mommy and Daddy and Jesus want you to behave—even when it's hard. Jason, what will happen if you are kind and remember to share while our guests are here?"

Jason grins. "I can take Johnny to the park tomorrow."

Mom smiles. "That's right, Jason, and not only will you please Mommy and Daddy, but more important, you will honor God with your behavior. Even though I am certain you will behave, Jason, what will happen if you are not kind and do not share?"

Jason's grin fades. "I won't be able to go to the park, and I will also have to sit in my room thinking about what I did wrong."

"That's right, Jason, but I know that won't be necessary because you have really been learning to share your toys nicely." Mom gives Jason a big smile and an encouraging kiss.

Clue for Christian Parents

Jason's responses indicate that this line of questioning is very familiar to him. He is comfortable with being asked questions regarding his future behavior. He is also well aware of both the positive and negative consequences of his behavior, and he knows the choice is up to him. (It was obvious to Jason that although the outing to the park had already been planned and was not a direct reward for good behavior, it would definitely become a consequence should he choose to be disobedient.) Giving the child the power of choice is the first key element in eliminating parent-child power struggles.

It is also obvious that Jason is secure in the knowledge that his mom says what she means and means what she says. He can rely on her consistent, loving follow-through, both positive and negative! Such follow-through is the second key element in eliminating the parent-child power struggles.

It is important to notice that Jason's mom takes this opportunity to praise Jason for the good choices he has been learning to make. Letting the child know exactly what to expect from a situation, what is expected of him in that situation, and praising the child whenever possible helps the child feel secure and encouraged. This is the third key element in eliminating parent-child power struggles.

"Jason, you know what you are allowed to do in your room. If Timmy is doing something that is not acceptable in our home, what will you say?"

Jason looks serious. "I'll tell him that we can't do that here."

"Thank you, Jason. But how will you say it?"

Jason smiles. "I'll say it nicely, Mom. Don't worry!"

Mom looks concerned and asks, "What will you do if he doesn't listen to you?"

"I'll come and talk to you and ask you what to do," Jason answers brightly.

"Good for you, Jason! That would be telling something important and not just tattling for no reason!"

"I know that, Mom!" Jason said proudly.

Clue for Christian Parents

After clarifying her son's expected behavior, this mom is planning in advance for situations that might come up with a child who is not known to the family. This type of advance planning may prevent arguments and hurt feelings between the host child, who is trying hard to be kind, and the guest, who may try to take advantage of the situation.

Mom notices that Jason looks worried. "Is something wrong, Jason?"

"Mom," Jason says thoughtfully, "do I have to let him play with Teddy?"

Jason's mom puts her arm around her son in an understanding way and says sympathetically, "I can understand why you would not want anything to happen to Teddy, Jason. Since we do not know anything about Timmy, why don't we just take Teddy off your bed and put him in Mommy and Daddy's room."

Jason brightens with visible relief. "Thanks, Mom." He gives his mom an appreciative hug.

Clue for Christian Parents

Jason is learning to share his toys and knows he is expected to do so. But he wants to protect his special, favorite toy. His mom understands and makes an appropriate decision.

The mom and child are now a team working together to be proper hosts but are protecting a favorite toy in the house from the unknown visitor. This smart mom has demonstrated her love and understanding to her son in a way that is very meaningful to him.

"OK, Jason, Mrs. Johnson and Timmy will be here soon. Let's pray and ask God to help us be good hosts." Jason prays and Mom closes.

Clue for Christian Parents

Prayer is strategic in the lives of Christian parents and children. Prayer is a powerful privilege that cannot be overemphasized. Training children to pray in each circumstance of life is a crucial part of role modeling.

The doorbell rings. "They're here, Mom! I'll get the door!"

As Mrs. Johnson and Timmy enter, Mom introduces Jason, who looks at Mrs. Johnson and responds, "Hello, Mrs. Johnson. It's nice to meet you! Hi, Timmy!"

Mom suggests, "Jason, why don't you take Timmy back to your room? You boys can play for half an hour before lunch will be ready."

Jason begins to go to his room with Timmy, then turns around and says, "Will it really take thirty whole minutes before we can eat? I'm hungry now." Jason's mother says nothing but gives her son the Look.

Jason knows the Look and respects it. He knows when he sees the Look that he has been out of line. The interpretation of the Look is always the same—at home or away from home. The Look clearly states: *Stop what you are doing or saying! If you do not stop this very instant, you will not like the consequences!*

Jason understands. He just turns around, heads for his room with Timmy, and says, "Thirty minutes isn't very long. Let's play!"

Clue for Christian Parents

Parents talk too much and say too little! That's one reason our words become ineffective and do not bring the desired results. In parenting, giving a child the Look is worth at least a thousand words.

The Look is probably the best way to communicate with a misbehaving child in public. It allows your child (and you!) to avoid public humiliation, and it gives you time to think through the situation before speaking. This can help you avoid saying anything that you will regret later.

To give the Look, you must make eye contact with the child and maintain it. This is done without a word being spoken. The Look assures the child that not only was the wrong behavior noted, it had better stop immediately or else there will be unpleasant consequences.

Needless to say, the effectiveness of the Look is determined by your consistent follow-through if and when the Look does not bring immediate results.

In his room Jason shows Timmy some of his neat blocks, and they start building a big fort.

While they are playing, Timmy sees the model airplane that Jason and his dad built. It is located on the shelf above his bed.

"Oh, wow!" Timmy points with excitement. "Let's play with that!"

"I can't reach it by myself," says Jason. "We'll have my mom get it down after lunch."

"Oh, I'll get it!" Timmy says, jumping up on Jason's bed.

"I'm sorry. We're not allowed to stand on my bed. I'll ask my mom to get it after lunch."

Mom calls the boys to wash up for lunch.

Clue for Christian Parents

Mom has carefully thought through what might happen when the guest is playing with Jason. Jason is properly prepared and is able to handle the situation in a reasonable manner. He is firm but kind, like his mom. Once again, advance planning and preparation have paid off!

Jason stays in his seat at lunchtime, remembering to use his napkin and not talk with food in his mouth. But he becomes so excited thinking about the fort Timmy and he built that he forgets to wait until Mom and Mrs. Johnson are done talking before speaking.

"You know what we built?" he blurts out.

Mom turns to Jason, makes direct eye contact, and gives the Look. Jason knows that look all too well and is aware of the serious implications. "Oops! Sorry, Mom. I'm sorry for interrupting you, Mrs. Johnson."

Mom is pleased that Jason corrected his mistake so politely. She knows he was excited but is delighted that he is learning to be a responsible boy. She gives Jason a bright smile of appreciation.

Clue for Christian Parents
Without the parent's speaking a word, the child has been corrected, the child has apologized, and the child has been commended. Jason quickly recognized his mistake following the Look, appropriately apologized, and earned the silent praise of his parent.

A few minutes later Mom asks the boys to tell about their fort. With great animation the boys share. Their moms are properly impressed with their sons' achievement.

Clue for Christian Parents
Mom knew it was important for her son and Timmy to share what they had been doing, but *not* as a reward for interrupting. She just waited until that disciplinary action had been resolved with the Look, then asked about the fort and gave Jason her full attention. When you ask your child a question, it is extremely important to listen to the answer. In this way you are modeling good listening skills.

After lunch, Jason asks to be excused. He takes his dishes into the kitchen. Then he helps Mom clear the table. When things are put away, he asks if he and Timmy can go play again.

"Sure," Mom says.

"Mom, when you have a minute, Timmy would like to see the model airplane on my shelf. Could you please get it down?"

"I'll be there in a minute," Mom answers. She comes within a minute and gets the plane down for the boys.

Clue for Christian Parents
This mom is dependable. When she tells her son that she will be there "in a minute" to do something for him that he wants done, he knows that she will be there. She respects

her son, and she has earned his respect. Respect must be a two-way street between parent and child.

All too soon Mom comes in to say that Timmy will be leaving in ten minutes and they should clean up. Jason does most of the cleaning because he knows where everything goes, but Timmy helps some.

Clue for Christian Parents

An important way for parents to help their children understand time and the passage of time is to give simple instructions using a certain number of minutes. Begin with a small number of minutes, perhaps two or three, then lengthen the time after the child demonstrates understanding. Once again, consistency in teaching is the key to the learning!

As Timmy and his mom leave, Jason stands at the door by his mom, says good-bye and thanks them for coming. They wave good-bye and shut the door.

Mom gives Jason a big hug and a kiss! "You were really a good boy today, Jason. Thank you for being obedient and for using good manners at lunch. Thank you for apologizing so quickly when you didn't want to wait for lunch and when you interrupted. You are really growing up to be a fine young man. I am so thankful that God let me be your mommy. I'm looking forward to taking you and Johnny to the park tomorrow." Jason beams and gives his mom a bear hug!

Clue for Christian Parents
Earned praise is a tremendous encouragement for children. Your child needs to know that you have noticed the good things he or she has done. Your child also needs to know that when disobedience has taken place—even in public— and has been corrected, the incident is closed and will not be dealt with again in private.

APPROPRIATE CONSEQUENCES

The parent–child
power struggle when
the parents are the last
to admit the problem exists

Children demonstrate respect for their parents by calmly obeying them. Parents demonstrate respect for their children by calmly expecting them to obey.

JOHN ROSEMOND

Teach your children to choose the right path, and when they are older, they will remain upon it.

PROVERBS 22:6

JASON IN CHARGE

Jason has been playing at Tommy's house all morning. When Mom picks him up, Tommy's mom says to her, "Tommy was telling Jason about our trip to Disneyland last weekend, and Jason told us that you went to Disney World this summer. How was it?"

Mom looks puzzled. "We didn't go to Disney World."

"Well," Tommy's mom comments, "I wondered if it was true or not because Jason's had trouble telling the truth when he's been over here before."

"Jason is a very truthful boy," Mom says indignantly. "You probably just misunderstood him."

Clue for Christian Parents
Lying is all too common in children and should be expected. After all, God's Word assures us in Jeremiah 17:9, "The human heart is most deceitful and desperately wicked. Who

89

really knows how bad it is?" This includes the heart of a child.

Whenever an adult authority figure makes a comment that indicates a weakness in the character of a child, parents must take a serious look into the matter, asking the Lord for wisdom and discernment.

On the drive home, Mom asks Jason, "Did you tell Tommy and his mom that we went to Disney World?"

"No," Jason lies, "I said I *wish* we could go to Disney World."

Now Mom knows for sure that Tommy's mom just misunderstood.

Clue for Christian Parents

There are three main reasons why parents want to believe that their child is telling the truth even when another authority figure says the child is lying.

First of all, it's easier. Dealing with dishonesty in the heart of a child is a big deal. It takes a long time to find out what the real story is, who the child has lied to, and for how long; then parents are faced with the problem of rooting dishonesty out of the child's heart.

Second, it makes parents look better. Parents have more than enough insecurities and anxieties about child rearing.

90

No parent is looking for yet another area where failure might be possible. If the child is telling the truth, the parents look good, and that means one less thing to worry about.

Third, parents desperately want to believe their own child. Parents long to be able to trust their child. There is so little parents can trust in this world that it becomes more important than ever to them to be able to trust the child God gave them.

The Bible assures us that "a youngster's heart is filled with foolishness, but discipline will drive it away" (Proverbs 22:15), so parents will need to deal with the dilemma of dishonesty.

That evening, Jason's dad is in the kitchen helping Mom. "Jason said he went swimming at Tommy's house today," says Dad. "I didn't know they'd put in a pool."

"No," answers Mom, "they don't have a pool, but Tommy's mom said she let them run through the sprinklers because it was so hot."

"Oh." Dad smiles. "That must be what he meant. Or maybe he was just using his imagination. I've noticed it's becoming more highly developed lately," Dad says with fatherly pride.

Mom agrees. "Our Jason is so creative," she purrs. "Really, dear, he's much more creative than most children his age."

91

Clue for Christian Parents

It is never appropriate for a parent to excuse lying under the guise of "confusion" or a "creative mind" or a "highly developed imagination." Parents who believe such nonsense are really only lying to themselves! Other children and adults are not so gullible or readily fooled.

There should be a major distinction between creative stories told for fun and "telling the truth, the whole truth, and nothing but the truth." There is no way to overemphasize the vital importance of building honesty and integrity in a child.

Two days later, Jason's teacher asks to see Mom after school. As they sit down, the teacher explains that one of the classroom windows was broken earlier that day.

The teacher explains that five children were playing in the area at the time, and Jason was one of them. She questioned each of the children individually. Each of the four children gave the same story and said that Jason did it. When confronted by the teacher, Jason insisted that he had not done it. When told what the other children said, he became angry and defensive and accused them of "making up stories and lying."

The teacher explains to Mom, "I've had trouble trusting Jason's word in the past, so I'm tending to think he may have done it, even though I have no proof. The other four children are dependable, and I have never known any of them to say anything to me that was not true."

By this time, Mom looks red in the face. She angrily retorts, "My Jason is a good boy. He has never lied to me. If he said he didn't do it, then he didn't. Those other children must not like him for some reason. They are probably jealous of him." Then Mom stomps off in a huff.

Clue for Christian Parents

Denial is destructive. When your child is having a problem such as lying and you choose to deny that the problem exists, the problem will only get worse. The character quality will become more firmly planted in the heart and life of your child, become harder to discover, and take far longer to remove.

At dinner that night, Dad asks, "What did Jason's teacher want to talk to you about today?"

"Oh," Mom casually responds in an offhanded manner, "a window got broken at school today, and she thought Jason might have done it."

Dad looks at Jason. "Well, Son, did you?"

"No way," Jason firmly answers. "I wasn't even playing over by the window. The kids just always blame me for stuff. They wouldn't even play with me this afternoon."

The parents shake their heads, mumble something about unkindness, and make no further mention of the window.

Clue for Christian Parents

Isn't it amazing how fast children learn to get the focus off themselves and blame others for their own transgressions? The tragedy is when parents are sucked into the scheme and then fail to deal with the discipline issue that needs resolving. Parents need to be on the alert at all times, lest they fall into the my-poor-child sympathy trap when children play the blame game.

The next day Mom is in the school parking lot. She overhears two moms she doesn't know talking about the broken window.

One mom is saying, "Jimmy's mom said the kids all saw this boy Jason do it, but Jason lied to the teacher and said he didn't do it. The kids say he always lies. Jimmy's mom says

Jason does have trouble with being truthful, but his parents just don't see it. Can you believe it?"

Mom gets into the car. Hot tears of anger flow down her cheeks. Jimmy's mom is her friend. *How can she possibly say such things about my sweet Jason?* Mom tearfully wonders. *What kind of friend is she, anyway?* She blows her nose.

Jason jumps in the car. "Are you OK, Mom?" he asks.

Mom gives Jason a big kiss and a hug. "Yeah. I love you, Jason!"

Jason responds, "I love you, too, Mom."

Still sniffling, Mom drives off the school grounds.

Clue for Christian Parents

Adult authority figures do not take pleasure in pointing the finger at a child. A good teacher is a tremendous resource for a teachable parent. Such a teacher has keen insights into a child's behavior individually and as part of the group. That teacher's comments about the social and emotional behavior of a child can be a source of wise counsel and guidance.

It is particularly painful for a parent to have a child criticized by a friend. At such times, a parent must choose to put aside prideful defensiveness and discover the truth about the child, even though that truth might hurt a great deal.

It is far better for a parent to humbly choose to see the flaws in the child, accept them, and deal with them rather than to defensively deny the child's problems and ignore the people whom God is using to give warnings that could save both the child and the parent from years of disappointment and despair.

Q & A That Lead the Way

Q: *At what age should a child be held responsible for telling the truth?*

A: As soon as the child is able to speak. If a toddler is asked about breaking a toy, that little one should be accountable for answering truthfully. Proverbs 20:11 tells us that "even children are known by the way they act, whether their conduct is pure and right."

Q: *Shouldn't I encourage my child's creativity by allowing him or her to embellish the truth?*

A: No! A young child who is permitted or even encouraged to embellish the truth for the sake of creativity will develop a habit of distorting the truth that will become extremely difficult to correct.

It is also true that a young child lacks the discernment necessary to distinguish between when it is appropriate to embellish a story just for fun and when it is necessary to clearly give the truthful facts. You must not create confusion in the mind and heart of your young child.

Q: *How can I tell when my child is lying?*

A: There are several keys to discerning dishonesty in your child.

1. First of all, you must *want* to know if the child is lying.
2. You must be willing to face up to the reality that your child is capable of telling a lie.
3. You must be responsive to what adult authority figures say about the child, rather than immediately denying the unwanted information or defending the child without an honest, thorough investigation.
4. You must be sensitive to the reputation your child is developing in the neighborhood, at church, and at school. Does the child have a reputation for being honest or dishonest? A parent who wants to know can find out without any problem!
5. Unless a young child has become adept at lying and knows you are susceptible to the lies, a child may have difficulty looking you in the eye when lying. Look for other body language mannerisms as well. Discerning parents become adept at reading the signs.
6. Most importantly, you must ask God for wisdom and discernment day by day. In James 1:5, God has promised to give wisdom gladly to all, but you must ask in faith, believing that our faithful God will be true to his Word. If you suspect that your child is lying but have been unable to discover the truth, ask God to reveal any hidden or secret things to you that need to be revealed. It is just amazing how God answers that prayer and makes the truth shine brightly!

Q: *What steps should I take if my child is lying?*

A:
1. Ask your child to admit telling a lie and give you the specifics of the situation.
2. Explain to your child that lying is not acceptable at anytime, ever, for any reason.
3. Tell your child what God thinks of lying. (Such verses as Exodus 20:16, Leviticus 19:11, Proverbs

12:22, Colossians 3:9, Proverbs 6:16-17 and Proverbs 19:5 provide ample evidence of the Lord's
hatred of lying.)

4. Reassure your child that although God detests
lying, God loves the liar, and he sent Jesus, his
only Son, to die on the cross so a person can be forgiven of any sin, including lying.

5. Tell your child that you hate lying, too, because
God hates it.

6. Assure your child that although you hate lying
and will not tolerate it, you love him or her.

7. Have your child ask you for forgiveness for the
lying behavior.

8. Assure your child of your complete forgiveness.

9. Remind your child that you will know whether he
or she is truly sorry—repentant—because if so, the
lying will stop.

10. If the lying behavior involves another person, then
have your child also confess the specific sin of lying
to that person and ask that person for forgiveness.

11. Help your child confess the specific sin of lying to
the Lord in prayer.

12. Have your child ask God for forgiveness for the sin
of lying.

13. Share with your child the assurance of 1 John 1:9,
that "if we confess our sins to him, he is faithful
and just to forgive us and to cleanse us from every
wrong."

14. Have your child ask God for help in telling the
truth in the future.

15. Tell your child that God is ready, willing, and able to
help with telling the truth, even when it is very difficult, but that your child must *want* to tell the truth.

16. Reassure your child of God's forgiveness and the
chance to start over with a clean slate.

HOW TO REMOVE THE PARENT-CHILD POWER STRUGGLE WHEN THE PARENTS ARE THE LAST TO ADMIT THE PROBLEM EXISTS

As Christian parents, we know that the answer to our child-rearing problems is revealed as we soak up the Word of God and drench our families in prayer. Yet the temptation remains to handle child-rearing problems ourselves and only seek divine guidance as a last resort. By then the problems are fully developed and will take much time to overcome no matter how seriously we call upon the Lord!

It is so much wiser, easier, and faster to appropriate the powerful privilege of prayer together with the truths of the Word of God to deal with the inevitable bumps of child rearing before they become mountains of adversity.

Let's rework the lying scenario with Mom's and Dad's eyes open to the problem and to the wonder-working power of prayer coupled with the truth of God's Word.

MOM AND DAD IN CHARGE

Jason has been playing at Tommy's house all morning. When Mom picks him up, Tommy's mom says, "Tommy was telling Jason about our trip to Disneyland over the weekend, and Jason told us you went to Disney World this summer. I don't remember you mentioning that trip."

"It's because we didn't go," Mom says with sad disappointment. "I'll talk to Jason about it immediately."

Jason comes out of Tommy's room, and Mom first asks, "Jason, did you help Tommy clean up all the games and toys you boys were using?"

"Yes, Mom," says Jason.

"Thank you. That was a good boy. Please come here for a moment. I need to talk with you and Tommy's mom."

Jason obeys by walking over, but his gait is reluctant.

Mom realizes that Jason knows what's going to happen. "Do you know why I've called you over here, Jason?"

"Yes," says Jason, looking down.

"Jason, look at me and tell me why I've called you here," Mom says firmly.

Jason looks up sadly and says, "Because I lied to Tommy and his mom about us going to Disney World."

"That's right, Jason," Mom says seriously. "Why did you do that?"

"Well . . . I guess because I wanted it to be better than just going to Disneyland like Tommy did."

"You know that it is wrong to lie, don't you?"

Jason nods. "Yes, Mommy. I know that it is wrong because God says it is wrong in his Book and because you and Daddy and my teachers say it is wrong."

Clue for Christian Parents
Although you will always be grieved to discover that your child has lied, you can be encouraged as you ask questions and your child's responses reveal the godly training in the home. It is confirmation that the child is being raised "with the discipline and instruction approved by the Lord" (Ephesians 6:4). You can be assured that the training is becoming a part of the child's heart attitude and thought processes.

"What do you need to do now, Jason?" asks his mom.

"I need to tell Tommy and his mom I'm sorry for telling that lie and ask them to forgive me and tell them I won't do it again," Jason remembers.

"Please do that now," his mother soberly requests.

Jason walks over to where Tommy and his mom have been watching and waiting. He looks them in the face. "I'm sorry I lied to you about going to Disney World. Will you please forgive me? I won't do it again."

Both Tommy and his mom express their forgiveness. Tommy's mom gives Jason a hug. The four express subdued goodbyes, and Tommy and his mom leave for home.

Clue for Christian Parents

When a child tells a lie it is best to deal with the situation as soon as you are made aware of the problem.

This on-the-spot discipline lets the child feel the full thrust of his or her guilt and gives the child the opportunity to apologize, to be forgiven by those to whom he lied, and to be reconciled with them.

In a case like this one, where another child and parent are involved, such immediate discipline also provides a good role model for the other parent. It demonstrates that ignoring problems, defending a guilty child, and postponing discipline are not acceptable in parenting. It also says loud and clear to the other parent, "I am committed to molding the character of my child in a godly manner. I want to know whenever my child is disobedient, and I will deal with the situation ASAP."

The short ride home is very quiet. As they walk into the house, Mom tells Jason he must spend some time in his room thinking about what he's done. "I'll come in five minutes and talk with you."

Clue for Christian Parents
Remember, giving a child a time-out in his or her room means that the child must sit and think about what just happened. Playing, reading a book, and taking a nap are not acceptable alternatives.

Mom comes into Jason's room and sits down next to him. She asks, "What have you learned, Jason?"

Jason answers contritely, "I learned that lying can be embarrassing. It was embarrassing to have to admit my lie about Disney World to Tommy and his mom. I don't like just sitting in my room thinking about it all either, Mom." Jason looks up. His big eyes are full of tears. "I'm really sorry that I lied, Mom. Will you please forgive me?"

"Yes," says Mom, "but I am very disappointed. Who else needs to forgive you, Jason?"

"I need to have God forgive me."

"You may pray to God right now." They both bow their heads and close their eyes.

Jason prays, "Dear God, I know it is a sin to lie, and I am sorry that I told that lie about Disney World to Tommy and his mom. Please forgive me and help me tell the truth from now on. In Jesus' name, amen."

Mom asks, "Do you feel better now?"

Jason nods.

Mom gives Jason a big hug, and they leave Jason's room together.

Clue for Christian Parents

After a child has gone through the steps of asking forgiveness from the people involved and from the Lord, a big hug from a parent reassures the child that he or she is truly forgiven and now has a fresh start. This form of reconciliation finalizes the forgiveness for both parent and child.

That evening, Jason's dad is in the kitchen helping with dinner preparations. He says, "Jason said he went swimming at Tommy's house today. Did they put in a pool?"

"No," sighs Mom. "They still don't have a pool."

Mom then shares with Dad about the earlier lying episode. Dad listens with thoughtful concern.

Just then Jason comes into the kitchen. He looks at the downcast faces of his parents. He can tell that his mom and dad both know about everything.

"Jason, please sit down," Dad requests. Jason obeys. "What do you need to tell your mother and me?" Dad asks.

Clue for Christian Parents

The wise parent gives the child the opportunity to confess a sin before saying anything. An unwise parent will either rush to defend a child and almost put words of excuse in the child's mouth or will angrily lash out before the child gives an explanation. Neither approach allows the parent to discover what is going on in the heart and mind of the child.

God set the most beautiful example of how parents should confront children with respect and caring when he dealt with the sin of Adam and Eve in Genesis 3:9-13.

Of course, omniscient, omnipresent God knew what Adam and Eve had done. God is never surprised. And yet, the loving-kindness of a gracious God dominated the confrontation. With respect for his creation, God did not lash out with the inevitable, tragic consequences of their sin. Rather, God the Father asked each of his children to give his or her side of the story. Only after God had listened to their foolish excuses and half-truths without interrupting did he remind them of the tragic consequence resulting from their choice to disobey.

With tearful emotion, Jason confesses his lie to both his parents. He ends by saying, "I guess I am just a bad boy."

Dad says, "You are a boy who has made some bad choices. Let's eat dinner, and then we'll talk some more."

Clue for Christian Parents

The dinner table is a place for family conversation and congeniality. Ideally, it is a time to share with the most trusted people in our world, our family members. More than any others, family members need to be the people who take the time to listen with love and understanding. That is the goal, attainable only as parents model the fruit of the Spirit—love, joy, peace, patience, kindness, goodness, faithfulness, gentleness, and self-control.

After dinner, Dad takes out his Bible for family devotions. Dad tells the story of Daniel, a man who could have lied and hidden his worship of the true God but who chose to be hon-

est, a man of integrity. Dad talks about how important it is to be worthy of trust, to be a man of your word.

Then each one in the family prays, bringing praises and requests before the Lord. Each prays that Jason will learn to honor God with honest behavior.

Clue for Christian Parents

A time of devotions together as a family in a consistent, positive, loving, encouraging atmosphere builds a strong bond of love for God and family unity that is truly amazing!

The length of time needs to be determined by the age and stage of each child in the family. However, even very young children love to be included as part of the "grown-up" atmosphere of family devotions. Reading a story, discussing it, asking a few questions, and culminating in a round of family prayer provides an incredibly effective yet simple format.

After prayer time, Dad shares Proverbs 13:5, "Those who are godly hate lies."

"Jason," Dad says with conviction, "hide those words in your heart, and I know that God will honor your request." Jason nods and says he will.

"To help you to memorize these verses, Jason," Dad continues, "you may write them down before you go to sleep. Then each day we will read them together at family devotions until you can say them without any help. Then Mom, you, and I will all know that you have really hidden them in your heart."

Mom and Dad kiss Jason, and he goes off to bed early, without dessert.

Clue for Christian Parents
Any child who is able to speak and follow directions is old enough to memorize the Word of God and begin the practical application of biblical principles in his or her life.

Psalm 119:9 asks the *big* question that is in the mind of all Christian parents who desire to mold their child's heart: "How can a young person stay pure?"

The clear answer follows, "By obeying your word and following its rules. I have tried my best to find you—don't let me wander from your commands. I have hidden your word in my heart, that I might not sin against you" (verses 9-11).

Children who have hidden God's Word in their heart are children who carry the Sword of the Spirit and are able to fight off the daily temptations and trials of daily life with boldness, courage, and victory.

Two weeks later, Jason's teacher asks to see Mom after school. "I just wanted to commend you on Jason's honesty," the teacher shares. "Today a rock broke one of the classroom windows. Just as I was ready to question the five boys who had been playing near there, I noticed the other boys whispering to Jason, 'Don't tell her!' But Jason boldly came to me and admitted breaking the window accidentally.

"Apparently he was throwing a ball, which hit the rock that flew up and cracked the window. He apologized and said he would pay for it, but that won't be necessary because it was an accident.

"Later, I heard the boys giving him a hard time for telling, and I heard Jason say how important it is to always tell the truth, even when it is not easy. He said that he had learned this from you and his dad teaching him from God's Book, the Bible.

"Although I don't personally believe in the Bible, I do appreciate good morals, and I wanted to let you know that I was very proud of Jason today."

Mom thanks the teacher for letting her know and leaves with a smile.

Clue for Christian Parents

Hebrews 4:12 promises parents, "The word of God is full of living power. It is sharper than the sharpest knife." The memorization and application of Scripture in the home is Christian parents' most powerful tool in teaching their children to choose the right path (Proverbs 22:6).

At dinner that night Dad asks Mom, "What did Jason's teacher want to talk to you about today?"

Mom smiles broadly at Jason and joyfully recounts the whole story. Jason beams as Dad tells him how delighted and thankful he is that Jason is learning to be honest and that he is sharing God's Word with his friends.

During their family prayer time, Dad and Mom thank God for giving Jason the courage and boldness to be honest. Each prays that the strength to be honest will continue to grow. They also thank God for using Jason to plant a seed in the hearts of his friends, as well as in his teacher's heart.

Jason thanks God that the "Bible words" helped him have the courage to be honest, "even when it was hard."

PARENTAL SELF-CONTROL

The parent–child power struggle
when the parents are
too tired, too busy, or just
too overwhelmed

Our children are like mirrors—
they reflect our attitudes in life.

The godly walk with integrity;
blessed are their children after them.

PROVERBS 20:7

JASON IN CHARGE

It's Saturday afternoon. Dad finishes mowing the lawn just in time to watch the football game. Mom is still up to her chin in laundry. Jason thinks gleefully, *This is usually a great time to get what I want!*

Clue for Christian Parents
A child is intently perceptive. A child knows exactly when a parent is too tired or too busy to be consistent. Given the opportunity, a child will always take advantage of such a situation.

Dad is absorbed in watching the game. He does not notice that Jason is in the room.

"Dad, can I go to Bobby's house to play?" Jason asks from across the room. Dad is focused on the game and doesn't hear a word.

Jason jumps between Dad and the TV. *"Jason!"* Dad yells, "get out of the way, or you'll have to go to your room!"

This tone is familiar to Jason and does not bother him at all. Jason does not move. "But, Dad, I want to ask you something," he whines.

Dad's irritation increases. "If I have to tell you again to move, you're going to your room!"

Clue for Christian Parents
There are times when it is appropriate to raise your voice—to warn a child of impending danger, for example. But raising your voice out of anger, frustration, or helplessness lets the child know that you are losing control. And when a parent is out of control, the child can easily assume control.

"But, Dad," Jason pleads, without moving an inch.

"Oh, go ask your mom. The team is right in the middle of a good play!" Dad says disgustedly.

Clue for Christian Parents

Dad told Jason that if he got in the way again he would have to go to his room. Dad should have followed through on this consequence.

Your child should be able to trust that you say what you mean and mean what you say. A parent who makes idle threats is a parent who cannot be trusted. A parent who does not follow through loses credibility with a child. (That's one reason it is so important to pray and think through the consequence before stating it to your child.)

Jason goes into the laundry room, where Mom is transferring a load from the washer to the dryer. There are piles of laundry everywhere. A huge stack of clothes is waiting to be folded.

"Mom," Jason begins politely, "can I go over to Bobby's to play? I talked to Dad, and he doesn't see any reason why not."

"Well," Mom asks without looking up, very much immersed in her job, "is your bed made and your room picked up?"

"Yeah," Jason lies. Mom knows she should stop and check up on Jason but does not want to waste any time. She is already way behind schedule because of numerous telephone interruptions.

Mom continues working. "If I find it is not cleaned up, you will have to come home and go to your room, and you will not be able to play with Bobby for a week."

"Don't worry, Mom," Jasons responds. "It's clean."

Clue for Christian Parents
Parents are extremely busy people. Even at home, there never seems to be a convenient time to discipline a child, to follow through on an instruction, or to check up to see that the child is telling the truth. Yet building the character of the child is far more important than accomplishing household chores, talking on the phone, or even relaxing in front of the TV.

To be consistent parents who say what they mean and mean what they say requires supernatural strength. Only God can give the self-discipline that parents need each day to be consistent.

Although Mom has her doubts, she replies, "Well, if Dad says it's OK, I guess so."

Clue for Christian Parents
A child quickly learns to play one parent against the other. Wise parents take the time to communicate so their child does not establish this habit, which is so difficult to break in later years and can cause havoc for the family.

Mom quickly adds, "But don't be too late."

"No problem, Mom," Jason says, speeding out of the room.

Clue for Christian Parents

A parent should avoid such ambiguous terms as "Don't be too late." To a child that generally means "Come home when you feel like it."

Jason runs to get his ball and bat. He feels just a little bit guilty because his room is a mess and his bed is unmade, so he hastily throws the covers up over his pillow and kicks some of the toys from the middle of the room to the edge. "There." He smiles to himself. "That's good enough." Jason runs out the door and down to Bobby's.

Later Mom goes down the hall with a pile of folded clothes. On the way past Jason's room she stops to peek inside. "He didn't make his bed!" Mom sighs. She notices also that his toys are still scattered around instead of being put on the shelves and in the closet. She realizes that she should call him and make him come home, but it's so nice to have him out from underfoot while she's working that she decides to simply make him clean it up when he gets home. "And he won't be able to play with Bobby all week," she reminds herself.

Clue for Christian Parents
Each time a parent fails to mean what he or she says, that parent becomes more ineffectual in the eyes of the child. Actions *do* speak louder than words. Why should a child be concerned about the idle, empty threats of a parent when the child knows those threats are meaningless?

Sometime later Jason strolls into the house, tired and sweaty. "Jason," Mom greets him, "your bed was *not* made, and your toys were out all over the floor."

"I thought I just had to have the toys out of the middle of the room, and it's hard for me to make my bed better than that," Jason whimpers.

"Jason," Dad says, "you know how to make your bed better than that. You go get it made properly and put your toys away and do it now."

"Oh, awright," Jason says, stomping off, "but I still think it was good enough."

Mom yells after him, "Don't plan on doing anything with Bobby for a whole week!"

About an hour later, Mom and Dad go down to look at Jason's room. He is playing with some of his toys. Mom and Dad look around the room.

"Well, your bed is a little neater, and a few more of your toys have been picked up," says Mom.

"We know you can do better, Jason, and we will expect it next time," Dad adds.

Clue for Christian Parents
Whenever you ask your child to do something the child is capable of doing and then permit the child to do the task improperly, you are cheating your child out of a character-development opportunity.

Right after dinner, Bobby calls for Jason. Putting the phone down, Jason runs into the family room, where his parents are relaxing in front of the TV.

"Mom, Dad, Bobby's parents have invited me to go to the movies tonight. Can I go?"

In unison, both parents say, "Sure!"

Mom adds, "But then remember, starting tomorrow, you can't see Bobby for a week."

Jason runs back to tell Bobby the good news, "I get to go!"

Clue for Christian Parents

Once again, Mom has gone back on her word. Jason has already figured out (although Mom hasn't) that he will get to play with Bobby tomorrow also. There is no reason for Jason to obey his parents because there are no consequences for misbehavior. It's obvious—Jason is in charge of the family. Unfortunately, his parents think *they* are!

Q & A THAT LEAD THE WAY

Q: *Since Dad was just watching TV, was it OK for Jason to interrupt?*

A: No. A child should be able to wait until the parent is ready to listen. The amount of time a child should be expected to wait, however, is determined by his or her developmental age.

Learning to wait with patience and courtesy is a difficult skill. Waiting is particularly difficult to learn in a culture that encourages immediate gratification. Even so, waiting is a basic reality of life. Waiting is something people must do every day. A child needs to be taught the skill of waiting.

Q: *Should Dad have stopped watching the game to give undivided attention to Jason?*

A: Not in response to Jason's impolite interruption. Discourtesy should not be encouraged in this way. Jason needs to know that he is a priority for his dad, but that doesn't mean Dad will drop everything at Jason's command.

Watching the game was a high priority for Dad right then. He had timed his yard work so he would be finished when the game began. Dad deserved his son's respect.

Q: *Should Dad have asked Jason to watch the game with him?*

A: Dad could have suggested that Jason watch the game with him. Many fathers and sons have great times of togetherness while viewing sporting events. Even young sons love to be included in these "male-bonding" times!

Q: *What should I do to get my child's attention when I begin to feel out of control?*

A: We live in a world of words. There are so many words coming at us from all directions that they begin to lose their effectiveness.

116

Silence is a secret weapon. Many parents never discover the power of silence in dealing with a child.

When you face those inevitable times of feeling anger, frustration, or helplessness, silence is a superb alternative to speaking for several reasons: (1) The moment of silence gives you time to pray and ask God for help in dealing with the particular child-rearing dilemma; (2) the time of silence will cause your child to stop and wonder, *What is she thinking? What is he going to do?* or *What's going to happen to me?* and (3) the time of silent, prayerful thinking provides you with the opportunity to think through the disciplinary procedures without saying or doing something that either or both of you will regret later.

Q: *Should Mom have dropped what she was doing to check Jason's room?*

A: Not immediately. Jason should have been asked to wait until Mom had come to a suitable stopping point. This time of waiting needed to be appropriate for Jason's age and stage of development.

Then Mom should have gone to the room with Jason, checked it over, and then decided whether he could go to Bobby's house.

Q: *Even though Mom did not check Jason's room before he left, what should she have done when she did check it and found it was far from satisfactory?*

A: Mom should have done exactly what she had said she would do. Mom said, "If I find it is not cleaned up, you will have to come home and go to your room, and you will not be able to play with Bobby for a week."

Mom should have called Jason to come home immedi-

117

ately. Once home, he should have been required to make his bed properly and clean his room the way he knew he should.

A time-out should have followed. Then Mom and Dad should have talked to him together about the incomplete chores and the lying. After a time of prayer, forgiveness, and reconciliation, they should have continued to follow through on the "week of not playing with Bobby" consequence. Needless to say, Jason should *not* have been allowed to go to the movies with Bobby!

HOW TO REMOVE THE PARENT-CHILD POWER STRUGGLE WHEN THE PARENTS ARE TOO TIRED, TOO BUSY, OR JUST TOO OVERWHELMED

When you are tired and busy, consistency with your child is an impossible dream. For consistency to be a reality, you need to have the power of the Holy Spirit working in and through each parenting moment. Without divine help and strength, consistency is just not a realistic parental goal.

But consistency is so very crucial. If you follow through time after time and then decide to let up just once, your child will be looking for the next inconsistency!

Let's rework this scenario illustrating competent parental guidance and training in life skills.

MOM AND DAD IN CHARGE

It's Saturday afternoon. Dad finishes mowing the lawn just in time to watch the football game. Jason helped him do a few garden chores earlier in the morning. Mom is still up to her chin in laundry.

118

Clue for Christian Parents
A child is part of the family team. Even a young child can assist you for a short while with various tasks. Your child then has the privilege of steadily learning skills alongside you, strengthening the relationship between you, appreciating the value of work, and understanding the meaning of a "job well done."

Jason would like to go play ball with Bobby. He finds his dad absorbed in watching the game. Dad does not notice that Jason is in the room.

"Dad, can I go to Bobby's house to play?" Jason asks. Dad is focused on the game and doesn't hear a word.

Jason jumps between Dad and the TV.

"Jason," Dad says firmly and calmly, "please either sit beside me quietly or wait by the side of the couch. I'll be with you when this play is over." Jason moves to the side of the couch.

Clue for Christian Parents
No one likes to wait. It is part of human nature to want to be "first" or to interrupt to achieve a desired goal.

Wise parents slowly and steadily teach a child how to wait with patience. Of course, the length of time the child is expected to wait must be realistic. The age and developmental stage of the child need to be considered.

One word of warning: You must not make your child wait just for the sake of waiting. Ephesians 6:4 cautions, "Don't make your children angry by the way you treat them. Rather, bring them up with the discipline and instruction approved by the Lord."

The play takes longer than Jason wants to wait. He interrupts again.

Dad turns to Jason and makes immediate eye contact. With a commanding look of disappointment, he quietly says,

119

"Jason, you may go to your room and think about the poor choice you just made. I will be with you in ten minutes."

Clue for Christian Parents
Even though it means setting aside an immediate pleasure, wise parents will sacrifice the momentary pleasure for the sake of developing godly character in the child God gave them.

Following through on the consequence for misbehavior will never be convenient. Realize that the discipline of today is an investment into the Christlike character of tomorrow. Focusing on the future will give you strength and hope to keep on keeping on and on and on—even when you are too tired, too busy, and would rather be left alone!

In ten minutes Dad goes to talk with Jason. "Jason, can you tell me why it was necessary for you to go to your room?"

"Yes," says Jason, looking down.

"Jason," Dad says gently, "please look at me when we are talking."

"Sorry, Dad," Jason says, looking up into his dad's eyes. "You told me to wait, and I interrupted again," Jason recalls.

"That's right," Dad acknowledges. "And you know that when you are told to wait, you need to do so."

"I'm sorry, Dad. Will you forgive me?"

"Yes, Son. Let's pray and ask God to forgive you, too, and ask him to give you self-control and patience next time."

Jason and his dad pray together.

Clue for Christian Parents

There is nothing more rewarding than forgiveness. That is true for an adult and for a child. Teaching a child the proper steps to being forgiven by God and by man is one of the major foundational blocks that is a parent's privilege to help put into place.

"Now," Dad says, giving his son a hug, "what is it you wanted to ask?"

"I wanted to know if I could go to Bobby's house to play."

"Well," Dad says, perusing the room, "it looks like your bed could be made with a little more effort. Then pick up these toys you were playing with and put them away. Then you may check with Mom to see if there is anything she needs you to do before you go."

Clue for Christian Parents

Any child would rather play with a friend than make a bed and put toys in place. But requiring the child to do the best job possible will overflow into all areas of life. The Bible admonishes in Colossians 3:23, "Work hard and cheerfully at whatever you do, as though you were working for the Lord rather than for people." That is the goal for a parent to set before the child and model: doing *everything* with all your heart, as working for the Lord!

Organizing a child's room so there is a place for everything—books, toys, puzzles, etc.—makes it possible for a child to learn to be organized and to be capable of putting things in their proper place.

Jason follows Dad's directions, then goes to Mom, who is still busy with the laundry. "Hi, Mom! Can I go to Bobby's house to play? Dad says it is OK with him since I've made my bed and cleaned my room. Dad told me to ask you if there is anything you need me to do before I go."

"Well," says Mom, rising out of a laundry pile, "has Dad checked your room?"

"No," Jasons answers truthfully. "I didn't want to bother him anymore while he's watching the game."

"As soon as I sort these clothes and get the next load started, I'll come and check your room. You could speed things up a bit by putting this hamper back where it belongs."

"OK," Jason agrees.

"I'll meet you in your room in five minutes," assures Mom.

Clue for Christian Parents

Asking a child who is waiting for your time and attention to help with tasks gives the child a feeling of being an important part of the family team. Be sure you let the child know that helping with the task is not only lightening your workload but will also enable you to give the child your time and attention that much sooner.

Mom comes to Jason's room a few minutes later. A big smile spreads out over her face. "Jason, you have done a fine job in your room. I'm so proud of you. When Dad's done with the game, I'm going to have him come in and see what a great job you have done. You are really learning how to straighten your room all by yourself."

Jason beams.

"You may go and play now, but please be home by two o'clock. And, Jason," Mom pauses. "Thanks for waiting so patiently while I tended to the laundry. Thanks for helping with the hamper, too. That saved me some time!"

Jason runs over and gives Mom a big hug. "You're welcome, Mom. I love you."

"I love you too, darling! Have a good time!" Mom exclaims joyfully as Jason grabs his bat and ball and goes out the door.

Jason comes home a few minutes before two o'clock. Dad

is there to verbally praise Jason for doing such a good job straightening up his room. Mom thanks Jason for being so responsible in coming home on time.

Clue for Christian Parents
Praise! Praise! Praise a child for a job well done! Adults can't get enough earned praise, and neither can children. Praise is the encouragement necessary to keep on trying during the tough times! Wise parents are always on the alert for opportunities to give a child deserved praise. Why would a child want to defy parents who lavishly dish out praise when it is warranted?

After dinner, Bobby calls for Jason. Putting the phone down, Jason goes into the family room. "Mom! Dad!" Jason says excitedly. "Bobby's parents have invited me to go with them to the movies tonight. Can I go?"

"As long as it is something we approve of and it won't be too late," Dad cautions.

Mom gets up. "Let me talk to Bobby's mom."

THE COORDINATED COMBINATION

The media-homework-chores parent-child power struggle

*The best inheritance a father can leave
his children is a good example.*

*And you know that we treated each of you as a father treats his
own children. We pleaded with you, encouraged you, and urged
you to live your lives in a way that God would consider worthy.*

1 THESSALONIANS 2:11-12

JASON IN CHARGE

As Mom is serving Jason breakfast, she says, "Jason, when you are finished getting ready for school, you need to start on your chores. I am tired of emptying your trash and cleaning up after you all the time. You are old enough to do some of that yourself now."

Jason just nods. He's heard it all before . . . over and over and over again. He's busy looking at the back of his cereal box. *These action figures are really neat!* he thinks to himself.

Clue for Christian Parents
When you speak to your child, the child should listen, paying full attention. This includes looking at you and verbally responding when appropriate.

Not requiring your child to listen is actually teaching the child to be a poor listener. This lack of listening ability will, of course, be reflected in poor listening skills in the classroom.

Mom leaves the kitchen to get herself ready. Emerging from the bathroom sometime later, she finds Jason plopped in front of the TV set watching cartoons. Mom yells, "Jason, I've told you a million times that there is no television before school! Did you empty your trash?"

Jason does not respond.

"*Jason!* Are you listening to me?!"

Jason ignores her.

"*Jaaasssssoooon!!!*"

Clue for Christian Parents
Jason's mom is acting out of total frustration and anger. Not a good way to start a day! Jason is showing total lack of respect for his mom. Mom is trying to get control of Jason by losing control of herself. This doesn't make sense, does it? Yet a parent will try to get control of a child this way and will fail—over and over and over again.

"Yeah, Mom," Jason responds halfheartedly, his eyes still glued to the set.

Full of anger, Mom marches over and turns off the TV with vehemence.

Clue for Christian Parents

Allowing a child to waste time in front of the television set rather than spending it productively teaches poor time-management skills. And if your goal is to rear your child "with the discipline and instruction approved by the Lord" as commanded in Ephesians 6:4, you will discover there is very little on commercial television that is appropriate for a child to watch.

Many families prefer to build video libraries after careful screening and selection. The discriminating parent will be able to locate sufficient videos for the family's viewing pleasure.

Evening is always the best time to watch a video. The mental and physical labor of the day is winding down, and relaxation is in order. Some families have a video night each week when they watch an appropriate selection together. Naturally, popcorn and soda are part of the evening's festivities!

"Jason!" Mom screams, "have you emptied your trash like I told you to do?"

"You didn't tell me to empty my trash," Jason responds annoyingly.

"Yes, I did!" his mother insists. "I told you while you were eating breakfast!"

"Well, I didn't hear you," Jason answers evenly.

"That's the *problem,* Jason!" Mom continues full blast. "You *never* listen to me! Now it's time to go to school, and your chores are not done. When you get home today, you need to *get your homework done right away* and then do *all your chores.* Now *get in the car!!"*

Propelled by anger, Mom storms into the kitchen, grabs Jason's lunch, lunges for his school folder, stumbles into the car, slams the door, starts the engine, hits the gas pedal full blast, and—they're off!

Clue for Christian Parents

Jason's mom has walked right into a typical parent-child power struggle by arguing with her son. Obviously, Jason is exerting the most power and is in control of the situation. Jason's mom emerges as her son's helpless victim. Mom not only permits his disobedience in listening and following directions but also continues to train him to be irresponsible by making it her responsibility to remember his lunch and get his school folder!

Your words must mean something to your child. Your child needs to know that each time you speak, listening is expected—or else! Appropriate consequences encourage good listening skills in a child. Positive verbal encouragement for listening well and following directions is a highly appropriate consequence. Age-appropriate negative consequences for failing to listen and follow directions could be time-out and loss of a privilege that the child values.

Jason sees his buddies on the playground at school and rushes out of the car. Before he runs off, he takes a quick glance into his folder to make sure his homework is there. His teacher has really been getting after the kids for not remembering their homework, and he doesn't want to lose any of his recess time having to redo his work. "Oh, no! It's not here!" he mutters. Turning around, he yells, *"Mom! You forgot to put my homework in my folder!"*

Clue for Christian Parents
What was that? *"Mom, you* forgot to put my homework in my folder"?

Whose homework is it? *Who* is responsible for getting it done and getting it back in the folder?

Of course, when your child is just beginning school, it is necessary for you to oversee the homework task. *Oversee* means that you make certain the child develops habits that ensure the satisfactory completion of the work within an established framework of time.

However, a parent must *never* take the responsibility of doing the work and getting it to school on time. Even in the early days of school, the child must accept the responsibility of getting the lunch and/or the homework to school.

It is the job of a young child's parent to ask before leaving the house, "Do you have your homework?" If the child has forgotten, the child (not the parent) must find the work and put it in the folder. An appropriate negative consequence should follow because the child needed to be reminded.

Mom parks the car, gets out, and hurries toward her son, loudly complaining, "Jason, this is the third time this week you've forgotten your homework! I am really getting tired of this! You need to start remembering the homework!"

"But, Mom," Jason pleads, "if you don't go get it, the teacher is going to be really mad, and I'll have to miss part of my recess."

"Oh, all right," Mom says with a sigh. "But this is *absolutely* the *last* time!"

This is the third time this week Jason has heard that line.

Clue for Christian Parents
There is no need for Jason to assume personal responsibility for his homework. There are no consequences for his lack of follow-through. Neither is he being taught any organiza-

tional skills. His character trait of personal irresponsibility is being strengthened. He is learning to blame his mother when things go wrong! He is also learning that his mom will be there to bail him out of possible consequences.

When a child learns that there are no consequences for lack of personal responsibility and that the parent will rush to assume responsibility for the child and accept blame for the child's lack of responsibility, the child is given a tool of great power to use both in and out of the home.

Jason plays with his friends while his mom frantically drives back home. Just as the children begin to line up for class, Mom runs up to the gate with Jason's work. He grabs it without a word of acknowledgment to his mother.

As Mom drives home, she looks at her watch and thinks, *How can I be so tired when it's only nine o'clock?*

Then she has an idea: *I've got to start remembering to check his homework folder before we leave the house. This running back and forth is too exhausting!*

Clue for Christian Parents
All that Jason's mom is accomplishing is training herself to be more and more responsible for the responsibilities the school is striving to teach her son!

Some parents have even been known to *do* the child's homework. If it weren't so serious, it truly would be comical! But since the major reason for homework in the lower grades is to teach the character quality of responsibility, this type of parental behavior makes it impossible for the school to have a part in the positive training of the child.

As they come into the house after school, Mom gets Jason a snack. "As soon as you are done with that, go into your room and get your homework done. After that, do your chores."

Jason knows what his chores are. He even has a list of them

on his bedroom door: empty trash from bedroom, make bed, pick up toys, feed the dog, set the table.

As Mom begins dinner preparations, Jason finishes his snack and goes off to his room. Just before Dad gets home, Mom decides to check on his progress.

She enters his room to find a big mess of toys spread all over the floor. Jason is intently building some type of edifice.

"Jason," Mom says in frustration, "is your homework done?"

"I'll do it, Mom." Jason excuses himself by adding, "I was too tired. I've been doing work all day."

That's true, his mom agrees silently. "Well, now it's time to clean up for dinner and your homework isn't even done, your chores aren't done, the dog is whining at the back door, and the table is not set. Stop playing and get washed up. Your dad will be home any minute."

Clue for Christian Parents

If a child is having trouble following directions, it becomes extremely important for the parent to check often on progress. Giving the child an hour or more to "get it all done" is totally unrealistic. The unmotivated child who is not being held accountable will become distracted within a short period of time.

Then, because of time constraints, the parent is put in a difficult position. The parent must decide whether to help with the chores, do them for the child, or just forget about them. None of these decisions will build godly character in the child.

Dad arrives home moments later. As he walks into the kitchen, he notes that his wife is obviously frazzled. Nevertheless, he risks asking, "How was your day, dear?"

"Terrible!" she responds. "You have to do something with that son of yours. He has been playing all afternoon! His homework and chores aren't done again today!"

Dad is exhausted from his busy day, too, and needs a few minutes to unwind, but he goes into his son's room.

Clue for Christian Parents
No parent appreciates being made the hit man because of the disciplinary deficiencies of the other parent! Discipline needs to be administered as the problems happen rather than being stored up until the other parent arrives on the scene.

It is not fair for either parent to have to be the bad guy when he or she was not a part of the original scene. In such a case, the parent doing the disciplining will usually either be too stern or too lenient and almost always will be missing some of the pertinent facts.

Dad walks into Jason's room, saying, "Jason, your mom tells me your homework isn't done yet. I thought we agreed last night that you were going to do your homework as soon as you got home from school."

"I know, Dad," Jason says, "but I needed a little break. It's

134

not fair that I have to do homework after working all day."
Then Jason adds, "How come you don't have to do any
homework, Dad?"

"Because I'm older than you," Dad lamely responds, irritated. "The fact is, your mom is out there setting the table
and feeding the dog because you didn't do it. Your homework is not even done, and I'm sick and tired of having to
hear about it every night and argue with you. Now get to
your homework and get it done *now!*"

Dad abruptly leaves the room.

Clue for Christian Parents

Unfortunately, a child who has demonstrated repeated
irresponsibility requires close supervision. Until such a child
proves some level of trustworthiness in the area of responsibility and obedience, the parent will need to treat the child
the way a parent of a much younger child would do.

Sitting with the child, hovering over the child, and
setting the timer for tiny increments of time are some of the
techniques parents can use when either training a very
young child in the area of responsibility or retraining a child
who has been allowed to become developmentally delayed.

The atmosphere at dinner is tense. Few words are
exchanged.

Later, Jason claims the homework is "too hard" and that he

"can't do it." Jason gets the full attention of his father as Dad sits with him and nearly has to force him through the work. The time is stressful for both.

Mom does Jason's chores for him, complaining all the while. Jason goes to bed grumpy in a very messy room.

Q & A THAT LEAD THE WAY

Q: *How can I teach my child to listen?*

A: The ability to listen is an important life skill that must be taught and practiced correctly every single day. Proper listening involves looking at the person who is speaking, not being distracted by other noises or things, actively engaging in listening, and responding when appropriate.

To encourage listening, you should take the time to sit down with your child, look directly at him or her, and command the child's full attention while speaking. A wise parent will choose words carefully, remembering that the fewer the words, the better the listening. Nothing destroys listening skills faster than too much verbiage! A parent should also refrain from calling out instructions to a child from another room.

Q: *Is it appropriate for children to watch television before going to school?*

A: Teachers are amazed by the number of children who watch cartoons before coming to school.

The child's teacher expects to work with a child who is fresh and ready to learn. In actuality, the child may have already been up for three hours, eaten high-sugar-content cereal, and watched two hours of cartoons with varying degrees of violence in each one. Cartoons are never low-

136

key. Typically, a cartoon excites a child toward acting out aggressive behavior.

That child is ready for a nap, not classwork! That child's teacher needs a vacuum cleaner for the child's mind, not books, papers, and school-related materials.

What is a child to be thinking about? What is a parent to instill in the heart of a child?

Before allowing your child to watch TV, a video, a movie, or play a video game, you must calculate the effect. Will this thing, whatever it is, put into your child's thought patterns things that are "true and honorable and right . . . pure and lovely and admirable . . . excellent and worthy of praise"? (Philippians 4:8). If so, it has God's stamp of approval. If the thing, whatever it is, gives negative input, God does not approve. It's that simple—and that difficult. You are accountable to God for your child, so the choices about what goes into the mind and heart of that child become your responsibility.

Q: *At what age should a child be required to participate in household chores?*

A: Even a toddler can be taught to put away a small tub of ten or fifteen blocks after playing with them. You can use the opportunity to spend time with your child as well as make it a learning experience. For example, you might say to your toddler, "Are you finished playing with your blocks? OK, then let's put them away before getting something else out. This is a green block. Find the rest of the green blocks and put them in the tub." And so on with each color. The child is learning colors as well as how to pick up toys before selecting another toy or activity.

An elementary-school child should be responsible for picking up toys with minimal parental direction. If the child is old enough to get toys out, the child is old enough to put them away!

Adding chores that help the family—such as feeding a pet, making a bed, emptying the trash, and setting the table—is important to building the concept of the family working together as a team for the benefit of each member. Gradually the difficulty of the chores will increase as the child becomes more responsible. Making lunches for the family, helping with mealtime preparations and cleanup, vacuuming, dusting, cleaning windows, bathrooms, kitchens, etc., watering plants, mowing the lawn, trimming the hedges, and sweeping the walks are all skills that a responsible child can be expected to do with success as the years go by.

The alert parent will know which areas of household responsibilities are in keeping with the child's talents and abilities and will encourage more participation in those areas. For example, some children will never dust or vacuum to a parent's satisfaction but are well suited to working outdoors in the garden. Some children demonstrate an interest and ability in tinkering or repairing things but can't seem to wash a window without leaving more smudges and streaks than before they began!

The wise parent will match the chore and the child so the chore gets done and the child is successful. The parent is then delighted to give the child earned praise for a job well done! The child is making an important contribution to the well-being of the family (and knows it!) and is also learning life skills.

Q: *When is it appropriate to reason or argue with a child?*

A: There are times when your child deserves to know the reasoning behind a request. By verbalizing the reasons, you can teach your child how to reason and reach logical conclusions. Although your child may *request* the reason, the child should not be permitted to *demand* the reason. A child's demand is a definite sign of rebellion.

It is never appropriate to allow your child to engage you in any type of argument. You should encourage respectful questions but not permit disrespectful demands and accusations.

Q: *Should Mom have gone back for Jason's homework?*

A: No. If a child is old enough to do homework, the child must be responsible to do the work and take it back to school on time. Homework is a way the school and home work together to build the character quality of responsibility in the child. If your child fails to get the work to school, the consequence should be administered by the school with your full support.

Q: *Should Jason's mom have checked on the progress of Jason's homework and chores?*

A: Definitely! It is human nature to want to play and have fun rather than follow through on hard things.

Until your child has demonstrated capability, dependability, honesty, responsibility, and trustworthiness in fully completing homework assignments, you must either go to the child and check on the progress of the homework as frequently as is necessary or ask your child to bring the completed work to you for a final check.

139

Similarly, until a child has demonstrated capability, dependability, honesty, responsibility, and trustworthiness in fully completing chores, you must check on the progress of the chore as frequently as is necessary to ensure that the child is following through and that godly character is being demonstrated in the life of the child.

Q: *Why do so many parents find themselves using such phrases as "I've said this a million times" or "If I've told you once, I've told you a thousand times"?*

A: Parents who use such phrases are not consistent, do not follow through, and do not say what they mean and mean what they say. If your child does not obey instructions, you must follow up immediately with an appropriate consequence—even when you are tired or busy!

God will give the strength and wisdom necessary to be consistent, but you must earnestly desire to be consistent and ask God for help in being consistent. A prayerful, persistent parent is committed to consistency with daily diligence.

HOW TO REMOVE THE MEDIA-HOMEWORK-CHORES PARENT-CHILD POWER STRUGGLE

Many parents believe that rescuing a child from the consequences of his or her behavior demonstrates love for the child. In actuality, it is the parent who allows the child to experience the consequences of the behavior who loves the child enough to be concerned about his or her character.

Our precious heavenly Father sets a glorious example all through Scripture. When his people sinned, they had to suffer the consequences of their bad behavior. However, he forgave them when they repented and did not leave them or stop loving them in spite of allowing the consequences to affect them. So often, suffering the painful consequences of poor choices was necessary before there was true repentance in the heart of his people.

So it is with a child. The parent sets the guidelines. The child knows the standards. The child chooses to ignore or disobey a standard. By experiencing the consequences of disobedience, the child repents and the parent forgives. There is reconciliation between the parent and child. Because of the discomfort of the consequence, the child chooses to obey in the future. This is what is meant by letting a child learn from making mistakes.

Let's rework this scenario with Mom and Dad properly guiding Jason to build within him the character qualities of responsibility, obedience, and respect.

MOM AND DAD IN CHARGE

After Mom serves Jason breakfast, she sits down at the table with him. Together they thank God for the food he has provided. They chat together. Then Mom says, "Jason, you got up about thirty minutes early today. That means you have thirty extra minutes before school to do something. Thirty minutes is like one of your lunch times at school. What do you think would be a good use of this time?"

Clue for Christian Parents
A child needs to learn about time in comparative units he or she can comprehend. Using the time frame a child understands, such as a school lunch period, helps a child relate to just how long thirty minutes really is.

"Well," Jason says, thinking, "since thirty minutes is like lunch at school, I could do a *lot* of things. I could build my fort and I could play with my Legos and I might even have time for something else!"

Mom counsels her son. "Jason, those are all good ideas, but keep thinking. Remember that you, Dad, and I have talked a lot about time being a gift from God, and we want to use it in the best possible way."

"But isn't it good to make things like a fort or make something with Legos?" Jason responds. "I thought you and Dad like it when I make things."

"We do, darling!" Mom assures him, smiling. "But stop and think for a moment. When do Dad and I do the special fun things we like to do?"

"Hmmm." Jason thinks deeply for a moment. Then his face brightens. "I know, Mom. You and Dad do the things you really like to do after the work and chores are done!"

"Right you are! Good thinking, Jason. I'm proud of you. That is very grown up and responsible thinking. Is there anything you should do that is more important than building your fort or playing with Legos?"

"Well," Jason says, "my room's already picked up, and my bed is made. It's too early to feed the dog or set the dinner table," he adds, grinning, "but I could empty the trash."

"Great idea," Mom responds. "That way you won't have to do it this afternoon, and when your homework is done, you can have more time to build that fort. But since you are a very good worker, it is not going to take you thirty minutes to empty the trash. What is something else you could do that would be a very wise use of time and would be honoring to the Lord?"

"I know," says Jason excitedly. "I could read a story from the new Bible storybook you and Dad got for me. It's got neat pictures, too."

"Perfect," his moms affirms.

"Then I can be just like you and Dad, because I've seen you reading your Bibles in the morning."

"You're right, Jason. Even though we are really busy, everything in our day goes better when we begin the day by spending some time with the Lord in his Word, listening to what he wants to say to us. I think you are old enough to begin to have time alone with God."

Jason looks concerned. "Does that mean we won't have our family story and prayer times at night anymore?"

"Oh, no," his mother reassures him. "We always want to have those times together. This is just a special morning time for you and the Lord to be alone together."

"I must really be growing up," Jason says proudly.

"Yes, dear. You are." Mom gives her son a big hug.

Moments later, Mom hears Jason empty the trash. Then

she peeks into his room and sees him sitting on his bed reading. She thanks God for the gift of her son and for the wisdom God gives her and her husband each day to rear Jason "with the discipline and instruction approved by the Lord." She is eager for Jason to tell his dad about his first quiet time alone with the Lord. "Maybe we can play a guessing game at the dinner table," she muses.

Clue for Christian Parents

Time is a precious gift from God. A child needs to understand that the gift of time is to be used wisely and carefully. As in every other area in a child's life, your example is your child's reality and will set the tone for your child's behavior.

It is not unusual for children to want to be like their parents. If you want your child to use time wisely, you need to model good time management. If you want your child to develop the habit of a personal quiet time with the Lord, you need to model the daily priority of time alone with the Lord in his Word and in prayer.

Five minutes before it's time to leave for school, Mom says, "Jason, we will be leaving in five minutes."

"OK, Mom," Jason answers.

In five minutes, Jason and Mom are at the front door. "Do you have your folder, your homework, and your lunch?"

"Yes," Jason says with a bright smile. "My folder with my homework was right by the front door where I left it last night. I don't want to get into trouble because I don't have my homework. Besides, I really worked hard on this, so I can't wait until my teacher sees how much I'm improving."

"Good for you, Jason. Since we don't have to take time to get your things together, we've got about three minutes. I know that you like to take flowers to your teacher. Would you like to help me cut some so you can take them to her today?"

"Sure," Jason says. He loves bringing his teacher flowers. She always smiles at him in that special way when he does something nice for her.

Clue for Christian Parents

With proper training, a child can grow up learning to work smarter, not harder. Organization in the little things is a big key to efficient time management. Even a child will be able to understand that there is more time for "fun" things when the routine details of life are managed with planning.

Mom and Jason chat in the car about what Jason read during his time in God's Word. Mom also shares. They plan the "guessing game" to use with Dad at dinner. Arriving in the school parking lot, they pray together in the car. Each asks God to help Jason be a good listener in school, be kind to others, and do his best work. They also pray for Mommy's and Daddy's day.

Then Mom walks Jason to the gate and gives him a big hug and kiss. "Have a great day, Jason. I love you."

"I love you, too, Mom," Jason says as he goes off to play with his friends before school begins.

Clue for Christian Parents

Don't all parents want to send their child off to school in such a joyful manner? Both Jason and his mother part with peace and contentment.

Training a child to spend a portion of each morning's preparation alone with the Lord—even if it is just a few seconds in the beginning—is a major factor in rearing a child "in the training and instruction of the Lord." This training is absolutely essential for every Christian parent who wants to raise a Daniel or an Esther, a man and a woman of God who stood firm with courage and boldness because they knew and trusted their God in a very personal way! The better a child knows God, the more that child will trust God. But if a child does not know who God is and what God can do in a life, how can that child possibly have the confidence to trust God? And how can a child get to know who God is and what he can do in a life without spending time in his Word?

Praying together before school is such a practical way for the child to learn that God is in control of the day, that God cares about the events of the day, and that God is faithful to meet the demands of the day. Philippians 4:6-7 assures each family member that as everything is taken to God in prayer, with thanksgiving, "you will experience God's peace, which is far more wonderful than the human mind can understand. His peace will guard your hearts and minds as you live in Christ Jesus."

A day that begins with getting up late, dawdling, then rushing is a day that is already stamped with tension and confusion. The stress will show in the child's life at school. Schoolwork and relationships with other children and adults will reflect what went on at home. Ask any teacher, classroom assistant, or school administrator.

As Jason files through the door, he gives his teacher the flowers. She rewards him with that special smile he had looked forward to receiving. Arriving at his desk, he opens his folder to take out the homework he had worked on so hard.

Oh, no, Jason thinks. *I was so excited about my handwriting on my spelling homework that I forgot to check for my math homework! I must have left it on my desk at home!* His face falls.

As the teacher collects the homework, Jason lets her know that, although he has done all of his homework, he has forgotten to bring his math homework.

"Oh, Jason, that's too bad," says his teacher. "I'll give you another math paper, and you can complete it at the beginning of recess."

Later the teacher comes to Jason. "Here's a note to let your parents know that you did not have all of your homework today, but I also wrote a note at the bottom of it to tell them how happy I was to see your spelling paper looking so neat!"

Jason smiles. He sure is glad she noticed. *I wish I had remembered my math so I didn't have to do it again and miss part of recess,* he thinks. *Next time I'll check more carefully to make sure I have all my work.*

Clue for Christian Parents

Choices and consequences—in action! Jason did not do anything terribly wrong. He had done all of his homework but forgot part of it at home. Simply forgetting something is a normal, natural part of life. Everyone forgets! Should Jason have had a consequence? Oh, yes! The consequences of forgetting help a child to be more conscientious in the future.

A child who learns to be responsible for mistakes learns to accept consequences with dignity and maturity. A child who is rescued from the natural consequences of his or her behavior, time after time, will fall apart emotionally when confronted with a mistake if no parent is available to defend, rescue, and "make it all better." Sad to say, many adults were deprived of learning the skill of accepting responsibility for their actions, and they are still unable to accept the consequences of their behavior with dignity and maturity. Such behavior, in an adult or a child, is not honoring to the Lord.

When Mom comes to school for Jason, he gives her the note from his teacher. "I thought you checked your folder this morning for your homework," Mom says.

Jason explains, "I did, but I guess I was so excited about my handwriting that I put it in my folder, but I forgot to pick up my math paper from my desk."

"Oh, well," Mom says. "Mistakes happen. Did you have to make up the work?"

"Yes. I had to do it again at recess."

"What have you learned?" Mom asks.

Jason knows. "I need to check and *double-check* to make sure everything is there."

Clue for Christian Parents

Although Mom was sorry that Jason did not have all of his work that day, she was pleased that he accepted the consequence in a responsible manner and has a plan for the future.

A parent who is wise and secure in the Lord is able to allow a child not only to make a mistake but also to accept the consequence of the mistake without interfering. Only a parent who is really trusting the Lord can do this time after time. You will face situations when it will take total self-control to keep from rescuing your child—especially when it will mean that you may look bad. Even in such a dilemma, you must choose to do what is best for developing the character of the child and trust the Lord to be faithful in working out the consequences.

As they come into the house from school, Mom gets Jason a snack. Then she takes time to sit down and talk with him about his day. When his snack time is over, she asks, "What are you going to do now?"

"Well, first I'm going to do my homework." Jason smiles.

"Then I'm going to make sure *all of it* gets into my folder!"

"Good!" Mom says. "When you're done with it, please bring it to me in the kitchen so I can check it before it goes into your folder."

Mom begins dinner preparations. Jason goes off to do his homework. In about fifteen minutes Mom realizes that Jason should be done with the work, but she hasn't seen him yet. She goes to his room to find him sitting at his desk.

"Are you done with your homework yet, Jason?" Mom asks.

"I just have one more math problem, but I don't quite understand it."

"Let's take a look," Mom says. She gives Jason some hints on the last problem, checks the rest, and gives him a hug.

"Now, where are you going to put it?"

Jason responds, "Right in my folder. For reading, I need to read to someone tonight. Can we do that now?"

"No," Mom answers. "I'm working on dinner right now. Why don't you do your chores, and we'll save the reading for after dinner tonight."

Clue for Christian Parents

Teaching your child to be adaptable to your schedule trains your child to be flexible. As long as everything is accomplished within the allotted time, sometimes things have to be postponed until you can give the child your undivided time and attention.

Mom goes back to the kitchen. Jason feeds the dog and sets the table. "I'm done with my chores, Mom."

"That's great, Jason!" Mom encourages. "Dad's not due home for another fifteen minutes. Why don't you do some building on that fort in your room."

"*Awwwwllll riiiiiiiight!*" Jason says enthusiastically, giving a big smile.

149

Later, Dad arrives home, comes into Jason's room, and asks, "What are you building, sport?"

"Hi, Dad," Jason says as he runs to give him a hug. "It's a fort! Do you want to look at it?"

"Sure," Dad says. "It looks great. Tell me all about it."

Jason shares until Mom tells them that dinner is ready. They clean up and go to the table.

Clue for Christian Parents

How pleasant for a dad to come home to a happy wife and child! How sad for Dad when Mom dumps her overload of motherhood frustrations and makes him the bad guy with the child!

If all the members of the family are responsible for their own duties and follow through with prayerful, God-given consistency on those responsibilities, time together at the end of the day can be relaxing and enjoyable.

At dinner, Mom tells Dad, "Jason has some great news!"

Jason adds, "I also have something to tell that isn't so great."

"Great news and not-so-great news . . . hmmmm," Dad says, "Let's hear the great news first!"

Jason and Mom play the guessing game with Dad. All three enjoy the delightful suspense. Dad responds with appropriate joy and thanksgiving when he finds out that his son spent time alone with the Lord reading the Bible storybook.

Then Jason tells Dad about forgetting his math paper.

"Did you get your homework done and in your folder tonight?" Dad asks.

"I did my math, and Mom helped me with some of it, and it's in my folder, but Mom said I needed to wait until after dinner to read with someone, so I got my chores done instead," Jason recounts.

"That's good," says Dad. "After family devotions, we'll help Mom with these dishes, and then I would love to hear you read. We might even have some time to add to that fort of yours before bedtime. What do you say?"

"That would be great!" Jason exclaims, smiling.

CONCLUSION

Matthew 7:24 talks about the wise man who builds his home on a strong foundation. This is also true with parenting.

At a very young age, a child is capable of being taught right from wrong. It will take many years of learning for the child to fully understand all that is being taught, but a strong foundation of godly character can be built day by day into the heart of a child. Obedience, kindness, honesty, respect, responsibility, and self-control are some of the outward manifestations of such character development.

If a child has been deprived of this strong foundation at an early age, it is not too late to go back and strengthen and secure the foundation on biblical principles. It will take more time and be far more difficult than if done during the early years when the child's heart is softer and more yielding, but it can and should be done. Do not be discouraged! God delights in doing what is difficult, and he is a master in overcoming the impossible!

There are definite consequences for parents who make poor choices in child rearing. What are the consequences for the parent who chooses not to follow through after giving directions, the parent who chooses to let the child get by without listening to instructions, the parent who chooses not to be consistent, the parent who chooses to make idle threats, the parent who chooses to ignore bad behavior, the parent who chooses to make excuses for the child, the parent who chooses to "rescue" the child from the consequences of lack of personal responsibility, or the parent who chooses to allow the child to blame him or her for the child's lack of accountability?

Superficially, it is obvious that the parent will be stressed out and not enjoy family life as God intended. God ordained that parents are to be in charge of their children. Therefore, there can be no joy where biblical child-rearing principles are not practiced.

Sorrow is often the consequence for parents who choose to ignore godly wisdom in rearing their child. The daily sorrows and disappointments the parent experiences when the child is small will multiply and increase mightily as the years go by and become penetrating sorrows that overwhelm the parent with despair.

The Word of God is clear about the consequences of poor child rearing: Proverbs 17:21 declares, "It is painful to be the parent of a fool; there is no joy for the father of a rebel." Proverbs 19:13 warns, "A foolish child is a calamity to a father." Proverbs 19:26 lays it on the line: "Children who mistreat their father or chase away their mother are a public disgrace and an embarrassment."

But what about extenuating circumstances? A nonbelieving spouse, a messy divorce, a blended family, custody problems, baby-sitter woes, school pollution, neighborhood horror stories, etc.?

God's standard is consistent and never changes. But God is merciful and full of loving-kindness. Because God is a great God, the great I Am, faithful as promised, he can take the ashes of any situation in which you find yourself and make something or someone beautiful out of them. In Isaiah 61:3, the Lord tells us that "he will give beauty for ashes, joy instead of mourning, praise instead of despair." Furthermore, God encourages in Joel 2:25, "I will give you back what you lost to the stripping locusts, the cutting locusts, the swarming locusts, and the hopping locusts."

With the Lord God Almighty there is always hope! But in the rearing of children, when a parent has the choice, it is wise to adhere closely to the principles of Scripture and not waste a moment of the child's life.

SCRIPTURE INDEX

GENERAL INDEX